Legacy

The Belief in Immortality
and the Logic of Culture

Praise for *Legacy: The Belief in Immortality and the Logic of Culture*

"Robert Fulton, one of the founders of serious contemporary study of death and dying, reflects thoughtfully on the legacy of belief in personal immortality. A sociologist, he is at his best when he traces how adherence to this belief continues to shape many aspects of western culture—sexuality, language civility, charity, war, and morality—often in ways readers might not expect. Fulton helps us understand how the legacy of the belief in immortality makes us who we are, individually and collectively. No small feat."

Thomas Attig, Professor Emeritus
Department of Philosophy
Bowling Green University

"Robert Fulton, a sociologist who has devoted himself to professing death and dying for many years, has brought together a brilliantly incisive, inter-disciplinary study of immortality. He treats the subject anthropologically by analyzing the Judeo-Christian tradition as a culture complex. His multi-faceted sophistication is evident in several disciplines including history and historiography. Hopefully, Fulton's methodology will inspire comparable work on the Buddhist and Hindu traditions."

David Kopf, Professor Emeritus
South Asian and Comparative World History
University of Minnesota

"Dr. Fulton utilizes classic literature to examine the belief in immortality and the place of mythmaking in culture. The discussion of the relationship of semen to immortality may be inflammatory to feminist scholars. Fear not! While grounded in the past, Dr. Fulton considers other options and raises the possibility that we may lift ourselves up by our bootstraps with a more enlightened view of the past and the potential for the future."

Inge B. Corless, RN PhD FAAN
Amelia Peabody Professor of Nursing Research
MGH Institute of Nursing Research

"Whether you are a Christian, a believer in another faith, or an atheist, this book may open up a viewpoint on religion you haven't considered. In *Legacy,* Professor Fulton, a renowned expert in the study of death, brings to our consciousness elements of our western religious legacy of which most people are not aware. The belief in immortality professed by Christians is the key theme. Professor Fulton explores this theme while investigating many other Christian beliefs and pointing out his problem with them. He analyzes and evaluates the non-rational and rational elements in our personal and cultural legacy and discusses why he believes they are often distorted. You may not agree with his ideas, but they will arouse your curiosity and push you to clarify your own religious beliefs. I highly recommend this book to you."

Ira Reiss, Professor Emeritus, Department of Sociology
University of Minnesota

Copyright © Robert Fulton, 2011. All rights reserved. No part of this book may be reproduced or transmitted in any form or by any means, electronic or mechanical, including photocopying, recording, or by any information storage and retrieval system, without permission in writing from the publisher.

Published by
American University & Colleges Press™
American Book Publishing
5442 So. 900 East, #146
Salt Lake City, UT 84117-7204
http://www.american-book.com
Salt Lake City, Utah,
Printed in the United States of America on acid-free paper.

Legacy: The Belief in Immortality and the Logic of Culture

Designed by Jana Rade, design@american-book.com

Publisher's Note: *This publication is designed to provide accurate and authoritative information in regard to the subject matter covered. It is sold or distributed with the understanding that the publisher and author is not engaged in rendering legal, accounting, or other professional service. If legal advice or other expert assistance is required, the services of a competent professional person in a consultation capacity should be sought.*

Library of Congress Cataloging-in-Publication Data

Fulton, Robert, 1926-
Legacy : the belief in immortality and the logic of culture / by Robert Fulton.
    p. cm.
Includes index.
ISBN-13: 978-1-58982-812-4
ISBN-10: 1-58982-812-7
1. Christianity and culture. 2. Immortality--Christianity. I. Title.
BR115.C8F86 2011
306.6'3622--dc22
                    2011003056

Fulton, Robert, Legacy: The Belief in Immortality and the Logic of Culture

---

Special Sales These books are available at special discounts for bulk purchases. Special editions, including personalized covers, excerpts of existing books, and corporate imprints, can be created in large quantities for special needs. For more information e-mail orders@american-book.com or call 801-486-8639.

Legacy

The Belief in Immortality
and the Logic of Culture
by
Robert Fulton, PhD

Dedication

For my sons David, Evan, and Regan
and in memory of Professor Harold A. Innis,
University of Toronto (1894–1952)

'The time has come,' the Walrus said,
'To talk of many things:
Of shoes-and ships-and sealing-wax—Of cabbages-and kings—
And why the sea is boiling hot—And whether pigs have wings.'

Lewis Carroll, *Through the Looking Glass*

Table of Contents

Foreword

I wish this fascinating, compelling book had been available when I was starting college. It would have helped me understand a lot about how the world works—about life and death, religion, the importance of myth in society, as well as about our cultural inheritance, generally. Rather than offering answers to the many questions these topics typically raise, *Legacy* provides a historical perspective and leaves the reader to ponder the public beliefs and practices we normally take for granted. Best of all, the text is coupled with references so the reader can look more deeply into the subjects discussed. *Legacy* is a book to keep on your desk—not stuffed away on a bookshelf.

One will find this book a good read or, better yet, a book to be read aloud to a friend. *Legacy* is equivalent to taking several college courses under the tutelage of an expert who, in addition to a long and distinguished career, has lived and taught in many different countries. Professor Fulton is more widely read than anyone I know; he is also humorous, clever, friendly, and erudite. He has been there. He knows what he is talking about.

I hope this book is but the first of a series and that readers stimulated by *Legacy* will prompt the author to take on more topics that need to be opened to the light of reason. His long view of the history of humankind examines many of the ways we have come to know this world we inhabit, and questions how and why we believe and act as we do. A book like *Legacy,* that examines our unchallenged beliefs and assumptions, is especially welcome today.

I have had the good fortune to know Professor Fulton for many years. We were roommates for one week a year for twenty-five years in a men's fishing club that met each summer and allowed us to talk and share personal and professional experiences while pretending to fish. Later, he and I became members of IWG, the International Work Group on Dying, Death, and Bereavement. We have spent several weeks in China together. We have shared the podium in cities and medical schools across Japan. We have worked together in European countries, from Denmark to Greece. Over these many years I have heard this brilliant professor share his insights on everything from the origins of chess to the contemporary problems associated with the transfer of family wealth across generations.

I am delighted to know that Professor Fulton has done what many should do, but few ever do, and what is sorely needed today: that is, offer the reader a myriad of insights and a critical evaluation of many of the contentious issues that challenge our modern society. In his masterful overview of inheritance, Professor Fulton extends his analysis beyond the inheritance of tangible things like property and wealth to the investigation of the equally strong and perhaps even more powerful influence of intangible things like myths, beliefs, prejudices, and fears that are a part of our common legacy.

Professor Fulton has set a very high standard in *Legacy*. He has shared the richness of his mind and experience before what I know will be an admiring audience.

William M. Lamers Jr., MD
Medical Consultant
Hospice Foundation of America

Introduction

Ours is a paradoxical legacy. At birth we come into the world beneficiaries of a disparate heritage: biology and culture. It is neither an easy delivery nor a favorable prospect. On the one hand, our biological inheritance endows us with such transient emotions as fear, anger, sorrow, and joy, while, on the other hand, we find ourselves swaddled by a material culture informed by logical thought but also abounding in irrational ideas and mythic beliefs. Metaphorically speaking, we are caught between the pestle of nurture and the mortar of nature. Not only do emotion and myth constitute a substantial part of our human patrimony, but they also represent the nascent point of human development.[1] In contrast, abstract thought is a relatively recent attribute given the span of time that humans have occupied the Earth; it could well be considered the stepchild of the mind.

Human consciousness, it appears, consists of two contentious functions of the brain: one that embraces ideas or images that are essentially emotional or nonrational and one that

---

[1] Douglas S. Massey, "A Brief History of Human Society," *American Sociological Review* 67 (February 2002): 8. See also Joseph LeDoux, *The Emotional Brain: The Mysterious Underpinnings of Emotional Life* (New York: Simon and Schuster, 1996).

strives toward the empirical and logical. It might be said that the brain is an arena in which two antithetical worlds collide: that of the French rationalist Descartes and the American fantasist Disney: "I think therefore I am" vies with its opposite declaration, "I dream therefore I may not be." The English philosopher Bertrand Russell would agree. He has observed somewhere that we are unable to prove that life is not one long nightmare from which we have not yet awakened.[2]

Fifty thousand years ago a period of social change took place that forever separated *Homo sapiens* from our Paleolithic ancestors. It was during this period, an era described as the "symbolic" revolution, that the earliest gravesites were created and language emerged. Importantly, the acquisition of language allowed for the development of verbal memory and for greater competence in cognition and analysis.[3] The acquirement of language permitted *Homo sapiens* to engage in rational and abstract thought. This in turn enhanced social intelligence and gave rise to sustained interpersonal relationships as well as the capacity to live in larger groups.[4]

With the development of language, categories of perception were formed that made possible a conceptual model of the world. These "mind tools," as they have been called, facilitated still other mentations such as memory and the capacity to dream. This newfound symbolic culture allowed *Homo sapiens* to synthesize these autonomous mental creations with temporal events and meld them into a coherent account to explain the creation of the world as well as humankind's place in it.[5]

---

[2] R. E. Egner and L. E. Dennon, eds., *The Basic Writings of Bertrand Russell* (New York: Simon and Shuster, 1967).

[3] Massey, "A Brief History," 20.

[4] Massey, "A Brief History," 9.

[5] Massey, "A Brief History," 9.

Every society has a myth about its origins. In its fullness it will explain the creation of the world as the work of a creator or a creatrix, a giant, or sometimes even an animal, who, for its own inscrutable reasons, creates life out of chaos or the primordial void. Such a creation story often includes doubt or regret on the part of the creator as a result of disgust for the creation or for humanity's moral failings. In creation stories of this nature, there is a cleansing of the world by a great flood. However, a particular man of unusual merit (with his wife) is typically chosen by the creator to survive the ordeal of the redemptive waters in order to provide the seeds of renewal while the rest of humanity is condemned to perish in the deluge. Such a flood-hero is called Utnapishtim (Sumerian), Manu (Hindi), Deucalion (Greek), and in the Judaic world, Noah.[6]

In creation myths that involve multiple gods, the story will often relate a struggle between two gods in which one will ultimately prevail. The vanquished god is subsequently hurled into the abyss but continues, nevertheless, to be a persistent adversary and threat to the victor's authority. In response to this everlasting challenge, the triumphant god institutes a moral code that is incumbent upon all to honor and observe if life—both mortal and immortal—is to be preserved.

The Judeo-Christian legend of creation is of this latter class of myth. With its belief in a Supreme Being, a hierarchy of personages in a *Great Chain of Being* bound together by *Natural Law* in a morally constrained, time-limited world, it provides an explanation for the existence of the world as well as the origin of death.

In their book, *A Dictionary of Creation Myths,* Leeming and Leeming propose that the myth becomes a symbolic model for

---

[6] David Leeming and Margaret Leeming, *A Dictionary of Creation Myths* (Oxford: Oxford University Press. 1994), 95.

Christian society's worldview—it's *weltanschauung*—"a model that is reflected in such other areas of experience as ritual, cultural heroes, ethics and even art and architecture."[7]

The conceptualization of the Judeo-Christian w*eltanschauung* is unarguably one of humankind's greatest intellectual and emotionally satisfying accomplishments. This worldview, moreover, fused as it is with moral imperatives, has been sustained and fostered in a world-embracing institution, the Holy Roman Catholic Church, which has won the confidence and fealty of an untold number of people for over 2,000 years. Finally, such a worldview offers to the faithful the promise of physical resurrection after death and eternal life—immortality.

It is the thesis of *Legacy* that the Christian belief in immortality is the *primum mobile* around which has evolved an elaborate *culture complex* (to be discussed in chapter 2). The book has been arranged in the manner of separate essays that examine different components of this complex—namely, war, language, civility, charity, death, and the belief in immortality. In doing so, I hope to explicate the influence that this belief in immortality has had and continues to have in the modern secular world. While many today challenge the concept of immortality as rationally unsupportable, its influence, nevertheless, has been profound and continues to be a pivotal idea in the temporal world of human affairs, despite the extraordinary advances of modern science and the emergence of urban, secular life.

In this book, my use of the term *myth* follows the definition in Webster's *New Twentieth Century Dictionary*, to wit: "A traditional story of unknown authorship ostensibly with a historical basis but serving usually to explain some phenomenon of nature, the origin of man, or the customs, institutions,

---

[7] Leeming and Leeming, *A Dictionary of Creation Myths,* vii.

religious rites, etc. of a people: myth usually involves exploits of gods and heroes."[8]

The philosophical position that I take in *Legacy* holds that the mythic tradition attends to matters concerned with the unknown. I share the viewpoint of the English sociologist Herbert Spencer, who contended that these matters are also—in all probability—unknowable. Modern science challenges the mythic tradition and its social construction of reality on the scientific grounds that as a set of nonverifiable statements beyond the reach of empirical testing, they cannot—within the canons of science—lay claim to being factual. It is my intention, therefore, to discuss the belief in immortality simply in terms of "as if." That is, one can neither deny nor dismiss such a belief; its truth or falsity has not been scientifically established. I would contend, simply, that if something is believed to be true, it is true in its consequences. *Legacy* discusses what some of the consequences are for the belief in immortality—both beneficial and nonbeneficial—for the Christian faithful and nonfaithful alike.

To understand the nature of our human psyche and the world in which we live requires that we not only acknowledge the presence of myth and emotion in our personal and collective lives but that we also recognize the significance and magnitude of each.

Douglas Massey, in his 2001 presidential address to the American Sociological Association, voiced a similar opinion when he observed that we have "unwisely elevated the rational over the emotional in attempting to understand and explain human behavior."[9]

---

[8] *Webster's New Twentieth Century Dictionary,* unabridged, 2nd ed. (New York: World, 1971), 1190.

[9] Massey, "A Brief History," 2.

He argues that what makes us human is the combination of our basic emotional nature with our rational mind and that rather than pitting the one against the other, we should seek to understand the dynamic interplay between the two. Massey maintains that our contemporary efforts to understand human behavior as the result of rational decision making alone is not only misguided but also prevents us from fully understanding the nature of the human condition.

Specifically, Massey characterizes the two dynamic aspects of the human brain as, first, the emotional brain associated with the limbic system and, second, the rational brain situated in the prefrontal cerebral cortex. Although the two aspects of the brain are connected and operate in parallel fashion, they produce two different systems of perception and memory. Moreover, even though the neural pathways between the emotional and rational brain function in both directions, "the number of neural connections running from the limbic system to the cortex is far greater than the number connecting the cortex to the limbic system."[10] As a consequence, unconscious emotional feelings and rational appraisals not only exist independently of one another but, as a result of the asymmetry between these two neural centers, the emotional impulses are also much more likely to dominate than vice versa.[11]

Rationality, Massey states, emerged very late in human evolution. Although modern human beings appeared over 150,000 years ago, it took 100,000 years for symbolic thought to evolve and another 45,000 years for speech to be systematized in writing and for a nascent rational culture to emerge. Even then, he observes, it has taken another 5,000 years for the

---

[10] Massey, "A Brief History," 17.
[11] Massey, "A Brief History."

possibility that a mass society could be established on the basis of rationality.[12]

Emotionality, Massey argues, is a strong and independent force in human affairs; rationality, on the other hand, is a recent fragile emergent. We are, he insists, ill advised to model human decisions, behaviors, or social structures as a function of rationality alone; rather, if we are to round out our view of human behavior, we need to have a better understanding of the nature and working of the emotional brain, which, as he states, "remains a strong and independent force in human affairs influencing perceptions, coloring memories, binding people together through attraction, keeping them apart through hatred, and regulating their behavior through guilt, shame, and pride."[13]

The conflict between the rational and emotional myth-making brain and its significance for our religious legacy has recently been addressed by two noted scholars. *The God Delusion,* by the English biologist Richard Dawkins, contends that we do not have to look to a god or other mythic power for ethical guidance in human affairs.[14] Rather, he argues, there is a prior basis to morality that is grounded in genetics. He maintains that kinship relationships display intrinsic evidence of reciprocation, kindness, and generosity that not only contributes to the survival of a species but also grounds the impulse toward altruism and the development of an expanding moral order. It is his view that the prospect of an ethical existence for humankind is immanent in our genetic structure and that morality is, fundamentally, an element of our humanity.[15]

---

[12] Massey, "A Brief History," 20.

[13] Massey, "A Brief History."

[14] Richard Dawkins, *The God Delusion* (New York: Houghton Mifflin, 2006).

[15] Dawkins, *The God Delusion,* 214–22.

As persuasive as Professor Dawkins is in contending that morality is a cultural emergent with evolutionary roots, one has to question whether he is not conflating nature's food chain and its species-specific codes of behavior with the belief in a *Great Chain of Being* that embraces all living as well as all mythical entities in a great moral network. I doubt that Professor Dawkins will find the alternative for our myth-based ethical system in the biological realm—*intra-special* codes of behavior are not readily translatable into *inter-special* ethical systems. I am hard pressed to find the prospect of any kind of moral agreement between the lion and the lamb that will be acceptable to both. I believe that the only time the lion will lie down peacefully with the lamb is after having had him for lunch.

It might be argued, however, that at the cultural level humankind's possession of reason has the potential to enhance the benign biological accommodations to existence noted by Dawkins. But a daunting chasm confronts us: the competing worldviews of the different national cultural religions with their profoundly different ideas concerning creation and the history-hardened nature of their unique social and ethical orders. Religion, according to the noted Austrian religious scholar Solomon Gandz, is nothing less than the soul and consciousness of the group-life of a tribe, community, or nation, and its function is to promote the cooperation of individuals in the interest of that particular community.[16] Simply stated, religion bears the institutional responsibility for addressing the problem of continuity or permanence in a society of which it is an integral and inseparable part. I believe that universal agreement regarding civility and right conduct can only occur when we

---

[16] Solomon Gandz, "The Dawn of Literature: Prolegomena to a History of Unwritten Literature," *Osiris* 7 (1939): 261–522. Originally published by Uitgeverij De Tempel, Bruges.

agree to a single ethical paradigm for all of humankind, which, given the divisive state of the world today and the role that religion has played and continues to play, is a most unlikely prospect.

The End of Faith: Religion, Terror and the Future of Reason by Sam Harris is a review of the conflict between religious faith and reason in the contemporary world. He concludes that the mythic views of life presently embraced by different faiths constitute the most dangerous threat to our continued survival and calls for their repudiation and abandonment. In this age of weapons of mass destruction, Harris is concerned—not without justification—that religious fundamentalists, who believe the prophesy of the *End Times* and with it, the destruction of the world, may unleash just such horror in keeping with their malevolent and ill-disposed prophesies. If we are to survive, he contends, we must uphold rationality and vigorously challenge such antihuman ideas. In his view, the many problems of the world that presently confront humankind will not be mitigated or resolved until we are able to assume a more rational view of the world and humankind's place in it.[17]

There is much to agree with in Harris's compelling argument. The Palestinian–Israeli conflict—the struggle between Muslim and Jew, for example—presently challenges the peace of the world. Religion and reason in this bloody feud find themselves in a death grip. The social, economic, and political needs of these two ancient peoples are at stake. Reason would seek a solution that is ethical and beneficial to both parties and one that would lead, expectantly, to a permanent peace. Religious zealots, on the other hand, relying on biblical revelations and prophecies, attempt to legitimize their *priority of sanctity*, that is,

---

[17] Sam Harris, *The End of Faith: Religion, Terror and the Future of Reason* (New York: W. W. Norton, 2005).

the right of one people to claim place and precedence over another. Regrettably, this stalemate is aggravated by those in the Christian community who support such an idea and cynically foresee in the full-scale eruption of the conflict the onset of the prophesized and long-anticipated war—Armageddon. It is their conceit that this war will culminate in the end of the world and only those displaying the mark of the Lamb (that is, Christians) will survive the cataclysm. They alone will be reunited with God in the New Jerusalem and they alone will share with Him the long-sought prize of immortality.

As appalling as Sam Harris's account is of the horrendous errors of commission and omission committed over the centuries that can be laid at the door of religious institutions as a result of their mythic-mindedness and as appealing as Professor Dawkins's contention is that ethical behavior can be grounded in something more substantial than unfounded myth and impenetrable mysticism, I believe that both scholars miss the mark. As I will argue throughout the course of the book, we are, by our very nature, myth-makers. We can do no other. The world as we find it is, in great part, the result of the manner in which our unconscious, autonomous, fabulating brain functions. To suggest that we abandon our mythic beliefs fundamental to our conceptions of reality—especially the belief in immortality—is to propose that we lift ourselves up by our bootstraps.

Each of the following chapters in the book illustrates how ubiquitous and deep-seated the belief in immortality is in the Christian world, even to its most secular parts.

The book is divided into nine chapters:

Chapter 1 discusses the belief in immortality through a review of the reasons considered to be of relevance to its emergence in human thought.

Chapter 2 examines the concept of *culture complex*, the theoretical construct that serves as the organizing principle for the book. By examining the annual New Orleans celebration of Mardi Gras, we can perceive the internal logic that informs its theologically based system of beliefs and related behaviors. As the different parts of the New Orleans celebration come together in a cultural complex so, too, do the different chapters of the book serve to articulate and reinforce the Christian worldview with its promise of immortality.

Chapter 3 discusses the role that the concept of the soul has played in the belief in immortality and the importance attached to its material vehicle—semen.

Chapters 4, 5, and 6 explore the different ways in which the Christian belief in immortality is expressed and sustained through the use of linguistic forms, the observance of civility, and the practice of charity.

Chapters 7 and 8 examine the belief in immortality in relation to war, self-identity, and death.

Chapter 9 discusses how the belief in immortality influences our individual and collective lives—both positively and negatively—to a greater degree than is generally acknowledged. In light of the different contemporary political and social issues such as war, the abortion controversy, and ongoing gender issues, the chapter calls for greater vigilance and a more proactive response to the irrational forces that assail us and threaten the good order and well-being of our modern world.

Legacy has three objectives. First, the book attempts to demonstrate the influence of the belief in immortality and the multiple ways it continues to be expressed in the contemporary world. Second, the book argues for the acknowledgment of myth-making as an innate function of the human mind and a fundamental part of our social and cultural legacy. Third, the book calls for the acknowledgment of the paradoxical role of myth in modern social life and challenges us to remain vigilant in defense of one of humankind's greatest achievements—rational thought.

Chapter 1:
The Belief in Immortality

O death, where is thy sting, o grave, where is thy victory?

—Paul (1 Corinthians)

He is no fool who gives up what he cannot keep, to gain what he cannot lose.

—Jim Elliot, martyr

It is a Judeo-Christian conceit that we humans are made in the image of God. Death, on the other hand, is made in our image. Death—the specter of a shrouded figure lurking in the shadows of our earthly existence—is anthropomorphic and understandably so. It is the individual who takes ill, sickens, and dies; who is killed intentionally or dies by misadventure; or who ends his or her own life by suicide. We humans inevitably die. God, however, is exempt from death; He is immortal.

Western history records, in no small part, humankind's struggle to be like God—to be exempt from death, to be immortal. This chapter explores the roots of this immemorial quest by examining the multiple ways in which the idea of immortality has impressed itself on human thought, such as archeological evidence, Judeo-Christian creation myths, the seasons and the cosmos, metamorphosis, delusions and hallucinations, mind-altering substances, near-death experiences, divine visions and apparitions, play, Greek philosophy, and dreams.

The gravesite at Shanidar, Iraq, carbon-dated to 50,000 BCE, demonstrates that our primordial ancestors buried their dead with ceremony.[1] Among the petrified skeletal remains, laid out in a symbolic, sun-aligned, East–West direction and separated by gender, were found items of utility: weapons in the graves of the men and personal accessories in the graves of the women. Also found at the gravesite were seeds identified by the researchers as flowering annuals—suggesting a belief in the efficacy of their regenerative power. Because such actions go beyond what is required to accomplish the relatively simple task of burying a corpse, these findings led the archeologist, Richard Solecki, who discovered the burial plots in 1957, to conclude that even at this early date in human history *Homo sapiens* believed in an existence after death. While paleoanthropologists debate his conclusion, there is little doubt that the gravesites at Geissenklosterle in southern Germany and those at Isturitz in the French Pyrenees, carbon-dated to 30,000 years BCE and containing musical instruments and other objects believed to be of service to the dead, offer convincing evidence of the longevity of the belief in an afterlife.[2] The presence of these particular grave goods, moreover, and the expression of emotions associated with death and separation that they intimate, could well be the earliest evidence of the sentient

---

[1] R. S. Solecki, "Shanidar IV: A Neanderthal Flower Burial in Northern Iraq," *Science* 190 (1975): 880–81.

[2] Richard G. Klein and Blake Edgar, *The Dawn of Human Culture* (New York: John Wiley and Sons, 2002), 195.

human mind of which we have any indication. Death, these ancient burial sites would suggest, is the midwife of civilization.[3]

Our understanding of human development and the emergence of early social behavior is enriched by the examination of these primordial gravesites. We are obliged to recognize that since time beyond memory, humankind has challenged the finality of death, and through ceremony, supplication, or sacrifice, attempted to deny our biological fate. If the evidence available to us is accepted, we are compelled to acknowledge that the belief in life after death—the belief in immortality—is one of humankind's oldest ideas, and, as I demonstrate throughout the book, one of its most significant and influential ideas.

The Judeo-Christian account of creation would have us believe that mortal death is punishment inflicted upon humankind by the creator for the transgressions of our earliest progenitors—Adam and Eve. We are assured in the account, however, that death is not natural to humankind. In the Garden of Eden, where God caused Adam and Eve to live, stood not only the tree of knowledge of good and evil but also the tree of life.[4] He instructed Adam and Eve to eat freely of every tree in the garden except the tree of knowledge, "for in the day that you eat of it you shall die."[5] Tempted by the vanquished god— Satan—in the shape of a serpent, Eve ate the fruit of the tree of knowledge and shared it with Adam. Learning of this transgression, God cursed the serpent and said to the woman, "in pain you shall bring forth children"; and to Adam, "cursed is the ground because of you, in toil you shall eat of it all the days

---

[3] Robert Pogue Harrison, *The Dominion of the Dead* (Chicago: University of Chicago Press, 2003), 23–25.

[4] The Holy Bible: Revised Standard Version, New York: Thomas Nelson & Sons, 1946. Genesis 2:9

[5] Genesis 2:17.

of your life.... In the sweat of your face you shall eat bread till you return to the ground, for out of it you were taken, you are dust, and to dust you shall return."[6] He then banished the couple from the garden in order to prevent them from eating from the tree of life, thus denying them immortality.[7]

The defiant taunt of the apostle Paul (I Corinthians): "O death, where is thy sting, o grave, where is thy victory?" can be appreciated for what it is—a taunt flung in the face of death in the confidence of his newfound belief in Christianity and its promise of resurrection. While Paul was put to death at the hands of the Roman emperor, Nero, in 62 CE, his passionate conviction of surviving death and ultimately being reunited with God has been embraced these past two millennia by countless millions of devout followers throughout the world.

But there are other reasons in addition to the biblical account why the belief in a continued existence after death is widely embraced, an idea that is all but universal and that predates the canonical formula of Christianity by tens of thousands of years.

For instance, the phases of the moon and stars and, particularly, the orderly progression of the seasons invite such a conviction. Moreover, to view a tree in the depth of winter bare of its foliage, only to witness its leafing in the spring, is to open oneself to the idea that all life is a cycle—an eternal return.

A further intimation of transformation and unquenchable life is the biological phenomenon, metamorphosis. To observe a caterpillar weave a chrysalis and later watch it emerge as a butterfly not only challenges the idea of death's finality, but it opens up the prospect of transcendent transformation. Metamorphosis, particularly of the butterfly, has not been lost on humanity. In Japan, for example, a historic ritual is observed

---

[6] Genesis 3:22–24.
[7] Genesis 3:22.

at the coronation of the emperor—the ceremonial donning of a unique kimono, called the butterfly robe—an exquisitely brocaded garment resplendent with multiple images of butterflies. For the Japanese, the symbolism of the robe is as plain to see as the robe is beautiful.

The annual shedding of the skin of a snake and the yearly loss and regrowth of antlers of different species of animals are further examples from nature that have also been extensively embraced as evidence of eternal regeneration. It needs to be recalled that in the New Testament, Jesus employed the analogy of a naked seed that, when planted in the spring, emerges in the fall as a shining new husk, to illustrate the truth of His teachings. So, too, has the mythical phoenix long served as a symbol of rebirth with its periodic immolation and subsequent reemergence from the ashes of its funeral pyre.

There are psychological phenomena that have contributed to humankind's rejection of the finality of death that need to be acknowledged: personal delusions and hallucinations. In the first instance, a person can believe, despite all evidence to the contrary, that a dead person is alive, while in the second instance, the person who experiences a hallucination can imagine he or she is seeing, hearing, or feeling the presence of the deceased.

Mind-altering drugs such as opium, hashish, peyote, and alcohol have contributed to the belief in life after death or the presence of another world. Throughout recorded history, human beings have believed that through the use of narcotics a transcendental world could be experienced and its incorporeal nature revealed.

Contemporary accounts of the so-called near-death experience (NDE) reflect this same belief in immortality. Vivid and compelling reports by persons who have purported to have died and subsequently returned to life add to the conviction that there is life after death. Such accounts are generally similar in outline. Having experienced a heart attack or been the victim of an accident, a person will report, prototypically, an overwhelming feeling of peace and well-being; being out of one's body; being propelled through darkness (frequently described as a tunnel); emerging into a golden light; encountering and having a dialogue with a being of light (at which time one's fate may apparently be decided); experiencing a panoramic view of one's life; being engulfed in a world of unearthly beauty; and meeting and communicating with the spirit of a deceased loved one.[8]

It is emphasized by researchers that not everyone who reports an NDE describes or experiences these different elements. The majority of accounts, however, include several, if not most, of the features identified and, importantly, they are reported to be woven together in a coherent and meaningful way. It is further claimed that NDEs have a quality of exceptional reality about them and thus are not perceived by the subjects as a dream, fantasy, or hallucination. Finally, the NDE is reported to have a profound emotional and/or spiritual impact on the subject, including the subsequent absence of the fear of death. It is claimed, moreover, that the experience for a nonreligious person can be a spiritual turning point in his or her life.

History is replete with reports of persons who have claimed to have had encounters with ghosts or who have experienced apparitions of divine or other otherworldly personages. In 1531, for instance, it was reported that an apparition of the Virgin Mary appeared to a native man of Guadalupe Hidalgo, Mexico, following which a church was built in Her honor. Known today

---

[8] Bruce Greyson and Charles P. Flynn, eds., *The Near-Death Experience: Problems, Prospects, Perspectives* (Springfield, IL: Charles C. Thomas, 1984).

as the Virgin of Guadalupe, She was made the patroness and protector of New Spain in 1754, and in 1810 became the symbol of Mexican independence. Today Her shrine—the holiest in Mexico—is visited by hundreds of thousands of pilgrims yearly.[9]

In 1858, a young girl by the name of Marie-Bernarde Soubirous reported having seen a vision of the Virgin Mary, who identified herself with the words, "I am the Immaculate Conception." Despite strong opposition, Marie-Bernarde was steadfast in her belief in the authenticity of her experience. Frail in health and desirous to escape public attention, she joined an order of nuns and passed her remaining years in seclusion. She lived in almost constant sickness and pain and died in agony. She accepted her great sufferings, willingly, fulfilling the Virgin's request for penance. In 1933, she was canonized by Pope Pius XI. The shrine of Lourdes, visited yearly by countless numbers of the faithful in search of a cure or relief from pain, was erected in her honor as testimony to her faith.[10]

Perhaps the most well known of all such accounts of visions in the Western world is that of the young French girl, Joan of Arc, who in 1425 claimed that she had been addressed by the archangel, Michael. She maintained that he instructed her to rescue France from English domination, and to install Prince Charles, the presumptive heir to the French throne, as king. Although unschooled and untraveled, Joan, seventeen years old at the time, made her way unmolested through 200 miles of unfamiliar, enemy-held territory to reach the French court. Despite the determined opposition of Charles's courtiers (which included the ruse of disguising him and compelling her to

---

[9] "Guadalupe Hidalgo, Villa de," *The New Encyclopaedia Britannica, Micropaedia*, 15th ed., vol. 4 (Chicago: Encyclopaedia Britannica, 1984): 764.

[10] "Lourdes," *New Encyclopaedia Britannica, Micropaedia*, 15th ed., vol. 6 (Chicago: Encyclopaedia Britannica, 1984): 352.

identify him among a large assembly), she persuaded Charles to allow her to lead the French army against the English at the strongly defended city of Orléans. He did and she did. In 1429, Charles was crowned King Charles VII in Rheims Cathedral.[11]

Every French child knows the story of St. Joan and she is venerated throughout France. Along the Colonnade of Kings, at Versailles, her statue occupies an honored niche among the twenty-five French kings: from Clovis who founded France in the fifth century, to the last king, Louis XVI, who reigned until he was beheaded in the Revolution of 1789. Over the intervening centuries, St. Joan has become the spiritual symbol of France for she, it is believed—as an instrument of God—delivered the French people from their enemy.

There are other intimations of the transcendental, such as play. As an integral part of human existence, play serves to strengthen the belief in another world. In his classic study *Homo-Ludens,* Johan Huizinga asserts that the act of play challenges nature's absolute determinism.[12] The impulse for humans to play—to make a metaphor out of life and to make life a metaphor—introduces an emancipating element into our otherwise mundane and deterministic existence.

The relationship between play and the belief in another state of existence can be seen to good advantage in the game of chess. The belief in the transcendental—a world where transformations occur and immoderate powers are exercised—is manifested in several ways. It is seen in the metamorphosis of a pawn, which, upon achieving the eighth rank of the board, may be transformed into any other piece except that of the king.[13]

---

[11] "Joan of Arc, Saint," *New Encyclopaedia Britannica, Macropaedia.* 15th ed., vol. 10 (Chicago: Encyclopaedia Britannica, 1984): 225-229.

[12] Johan Huizinga, *Homo-Ludens* (Boston: Beacon Press, 1955), 3.

[13] This particular rule brings to mind the practice found in the military tradition of the battlefield commission. In this ancient custom, a common

It is suggested in the levitating ability of the rook in the act of castling, and in the unique L-shaped move of the knight, which permits it to leap over friend and foe alike. The expression of these extraordinary powers serves to imply a different and separate order of existence, where all things normally denied, or beyond the capability of human beings, are possible.

There is one more thing about play: play changes our relationship to the transcendental. When the emperor of Japan dons the butterfly robe at his coronation, it not only symbolizes the belief in the existence of both a temporal and trans-temporal world but it also lays claim to his authority in both; so, too, with play. We claim, albeit for a brief moment, authority over our lives. With play, the transcendental is momentarily dethroned. It is we who are the primary actors and it is we who establish the rules of the game. The arena of play is the setting for the acting out of human aspirations and it is here that the mundane world prevails and time itself can be commanded to stand still. At such moments humankind creates its own reality, is master of its domain, and the arbiter of its fate.

It is this illogical association of the transcendental and the mundane, I would contend, that gives the game of chess its unique fascination and historic appeal.

While the idea of the transcendental and the belief in immortality are simply implied in the practice of play, they were consciously and rationally argued by early Greek philosophers. In his Ingersoll lecture for 1958, an annual lectureship on immortality sponsored by Harvard University since 1894, theologian Werner Jaeger succinctly summarized the long and

---

soldier can be elevated to officer rank and thus to the status of gentleman as a result of an act of bravery or some other outstanding accomplishment on the battlefield.

convoluted history of this revolutionary idea in human thought.[14]

The belief in the divine origin of human life and an immortal soul, Jaeger informs us, finds its roots in the mystic cult of Orphism (sixth century BCE). For the followers of Orphism, the ideal of the ascetic life—the *bioc*—ensured the purity of the soul during its sojourn on Earth so that it would return to its divine home after death.

The early Christians developed a profound interest in the pagan philosophers, who taught that the soul existed and was immortal and not corruptible like the human body. This idea, Jaeger states, was particularly embraced after the apostle Paul made the resurrection of the body the cornerstone of the Christian faith. Although the Greek concept of immortality of the soul is not the same as Paul's vision of a resurrected or transfigured body, Jaeger observes, both ideas have a natural affinity for each other. It eventually transpired that the belief in the indestructibility of the soul came to be perceived by the early Church Fathers as foreshadowing their belief in resurrection. [15]

In the Homeric epics the *Iliad* and the *Odyssey* (eighth century BCE), the earliest of Greek poetry, men did not survive their bodies; rather, they went to Hades, a land of shadows without conscious life or mental activity that was located across the river Lethe, the waters of forgetfulness. During this period in Greek life, the belief was that all that survived of a man after his death was his name, which was kept alive by his reputation. For the great mass of mortals, there was nothing to hope for after death. For the valiant warrior, on the other hand, his name would live on in the memory of his celebrated deeds that would be

---

[14] Werner Jaeger, "The Greek Ideas of Immortality," Ingersoll Lecture for 1958, *Harvard Theological Review* 52 (no. 3, 1959): 136–47.

[15] Jaeger, "The Greek Ideas."

recounted in the songs of the *aoidoi*. In these songs, Jaeger recounts, "the great deeds of gods and men were equally praised; the difference between them seemed almost to disappear, and the heroic individual acquired eternal glory and reputation." For a Greek of the Homeric age, to be remembered after death by his fellow man was immortality.[16]

By the time of Plato (fourth century BCE), conceptual changes had occurred. Other men of the Greek *polis* (Greek community)—the lawgiver, the poet, the writer, and the philosopher—also came to be immortalized. The idea of an immortality intrinsic to one's self began to assume a greater place in the mind of the Greeks, even as the traditional authority of the *polis* to grant such a status was giving way to the recognition of the increasingly autonomous individual. At this point in history, Jaeger explains, a new view of immortality was embraced. By professing that the mentations of the human mind were "the innate metaphysical *eros* for immortal life" and having embraced the Orphic belief in the divine origin of humankind, Plato declared that the soul of an individual itself was immortal and separable from the body.[17]

There is, however, a more fundamental reason for the belief that mortal death is not the end of existence than the speculations of Greek philosophers. The simple fact is, human beings dream.

The brain's ability in the state of sleep to construct the phantasmagorical and the commonplace as well as images of the dead has had a much more profound impact on human thought through the ages than is generally recognized and is a significant reason for the belief in life after death.

There are accounts in the literature of widows and widowers who have experienced dreams in which their deceased spouses appear to them sometimes for decades following their deaths.[18] Moreover, a person who may have previously witnessed the physical destruction of a person (consumed by fire or devoured by an animal) may experience him or her in a dream alive and wholly restored. This mental product is analogous to what psychologist Marianne Zimmel has described as the "phantom-limb" phenomenon, "a somatic experience in which a person, who is missing an arm or leg, continues to feel its physical presence."[19] The importance of experiencing a dream in which the dead appear alive cannot be overstated. It serves not only to contradict perceived reality but also provides a persuasive argument for the existence of an unperceived transcendental state.

Since time immemorial, the dream has been understood as a window onto another world and has held a place of great importance in the secular and spiritual life of humankind. Indeed, the Western world owes its adoption of Christianity to the belief in the veracity of the dream. According to historical account, the Roman emperor Constantine (285–337 CE) dreamt that if he were to fight under the sign of the cross, at what came to be known as the battle of Milvian Bridge, he would prevail. He did, and he was victorious. Christianity was established as the official religion of the Roman Empire the following year.[20]

---

[18] Richard M. Griffith, Otoya Miyagi, and Akira Tago, "The Universality of Typical Dreams: Japanese vs. Americans," *American Anthropologist* 60 (1948): 1173–79.

[19] M. L. Zimmel, "The Conditions of Occurrence of Phantom Limbs," *Proceedings of the American Philosophical Society* 102 (1958): 492–500.

[20] "Constantine the Great," *New Encyclopaedia Britannica, Macropaedia*, 15th ed., vol. 5 (Chicago: Encyclopaedia Britannica, 1984): 72.

Appreciation of the significance of dreaming for the belief in life after death and its equally important role in human affairs, however, has been greatly diminished in the Western world since the publication of *The Interpretation of Dreams* by Sigmund Freud in 1901.[21] Given his rational perspective, it was his professional conviction as a physician that the religious impulse was a mental affliction, and he consequently jettisoned those aspects of the dream that to him reflected superstitious or other nonrational religious beliefs. For untold centuries, it had been accepted throughout the ancient world (Greece, Italy, Persia, India and Egypt) that dreams were (1) communications from the gods, (2) emanations of the soul, (3) forebodings from demons or ghosts, (4) intimations from the physical state of the body, and (5) chance accompaniments of events that happen in waking life, including things wished for or desired.[22] Freud settled on the single formulation (following his Greek precursor, Synesius) that dreams were unique mental products of the dreamer related to his or her temporal waking life. He emphasized the particular aspects of a dream that were distinct to the individual at the expense of the idea that the dream was also a semiotic message that would have meaning and significance for the entire community. In his twentieth-century enthusiasm for a rational science and his prejudice against any form of religious belief, Freud rejected out of hand the long-held conviction that the dream was an integral and meaningful aspect of social life. In doing so, he closed a window of understanding regarding the dream as having an historically

---

[21] Sigmund Freud, *The Interpretations of Dreams* (New York: Modern Library, 1950).

[22] Achmet, *The Oneirocriticon of Achmet, A Medieval Greek and Arabic Treatise on the Interpretation of Dreams*, trans. by Steven M. Oberhelman (Lubbock: Texas Tech University Press, 1991).

significant role in social affairs, even as he attempted to open a window onto the workings of the individual human mind.

Importantly, however, modern neuroscience informs us that contrary to what our ancestors believed or what Freud claimed, dreaming is neither; it is simply an autonomous, self-actuating activity of the brain. J. Allan Hobson in his recent book *Dreaming: An Introduction to the Science of Sleep* informs us that the brain, in the process of dreaming, is simply integrating information, consolidating and revising memory, and learning newly acquired skills. Although he agrees that much research still needs to be conducted for a complete theory of dreaming, this much Hobson believes: (1) waking and dreaming constitute two different states of consciousness that depend upon the body's chemistry and internal sensory inputs and motor outputs; and (2) the dream has no particular function in and of itself, but it presents to us, in sometimes startling and dramatic fashion, phantasmagorical images and other "fatherless inventions" of its own unconscious creation.[23]

Rodney Needham, the English social psychologist, speculates that the greater part of the dream material is probably an expression of one's cultural inheritance. In his book *Primordial Characters,* he contends that some aspects of the dream are so universal and inordinately unworldly that they cannot be ascribed to the influences of culture per se. Rather, he concludes, the correspondence between the dreaming self and the mental life of the greater society testifies to an aspect of the imagination that is a normal, if disorderly, function of consciousness and intrinsic to human nature.[24]

---

[23] J. Allan Hobson, *Dreaming: An Introduction to the Science of Sleep* (Oxford: Oxford University Press, 2002).

[24] Rodney Needham, *Primordial Characters* (Charlottesville: University Press of Virginia, 1978), 65.

Of signal importance is the fact that the same fantasies, images, and paranormal activities identified by Hobson and Needham as experienced in the dream state are also found in the waking state and together serve to buttress the accepted normalcy of such inordinate powers and mentations.

In the realm of children's literature, for example, one is not surprised or disturbed that animals speak or hold conversations with humans. The celebrated stories of the Brothers Grimm include the fable of the goblin, Rumpelstiltskin, who had the magical power to spin straw into gold. The tales of Mother Goose include a story of a cow that jumped over the moon. Lewis Carroll, in *Alice in Wonderland*, has his heroine, Alice, enter into a magical kingdom through a looking glass only to have her life threatened by a playing card. Contemporaneously, J. K. Rowling endows her hero, Harry Potter, with the ability to become invisible, conjure spells, and fly.

Paranormal phenomena are present in many other facets of Western culture and have been unquestionably embraced by the arts throughout the centuries. For instance, in Shakespeare's *The Tempest*, we find the presence of airy spirits and a magic robe, while in his *A Midsummer Night's Dream*, fairies abound while one of the play's characters, Bottom, is transformed into an ass. In *Hamlet*, Shakespeare has his eponymous character converse with the ghost of his dead father, while in *Macbeth*, witches and a ghost are encountered. Present-day audiences are neither surprised nor discomforted by such supernatural materializations in the works of Western societies' premier playwright.

Western painting, too, has addressed itself to the paranormal and the transcendental. God, His saints and angels, as well as His other familiars, have long been the subject of the greatest artists. *The Last Supper* by DaVinci, *The Last Judgment* of the Sistine Chapel by Michelangelo, Rembrandt's *The Holy Family* and *The Sacrifice of Abraham*, Jean de Beaumetz's *Christ on the Cross with a Praying Carthusian Monk*, Juan de Flandes's *Nativity*, and Caravaggio's *The Calling of St. Matthew* are but a few examples of this religiously inspired, other-worldly vision.

This vision continues in Western sculpture. Michelangelo's profoundly moving *Pieta,* for instance, portrays a mourning mother even more youthful in appearance than her dead son, while his majestic *Moses* appears before us horned. Such sculpture celebrates the Western belief in the transcendental and, by implication, the prospect of personal immortality and spiritual reunion with God.

In music, also, we find the majesty and power of the transcendental expressed through the paranormal. For instance, in Mozart's opera *The Magic Flute,* the character Papagano is endowed with a set of chimes and an enchanted flute that protects him from harm. In the opera *Don Giovanni,* the protagonist is sent to his doom by a talking statue while being mocked by demons. In Wagner's opera *Siegfried,* one finds the dragon, Fafner, and a magical gold ring, the possession of which allows the possessor to rule the world. In Humperdinck's *Hansel and Gretel,* the children are made prisoners by a witch by means of a spell. In Boïto's opera *Mefistofele* are to be found cherubim, witches, nymphs, sorcerers, celestial phalanxes, and sirens, as well as God.

In the realm of architecture, one is reminded of the great Christian edifices of the world: the cathedrals of Rheims, Cologne, St. Peters, St. Paul's, St. Isaacs, and Santiago de Compostela. One recalls, too, the mosques of Islam, St. Sophia and the Blue Mosque of Istanbul, as well as the Wailing Wall, the historic remnant of Solomon's temple in Jerusalem. By their great antiquity, historical importance, and commanding presence, such sacred sanctuaries are architectural proclamations that testify not only to the belief in a transcendental order but also give tangible substance to the belief in a life eternal.

Poets, too, since the time of the composition of the epic *Gilgamesh* have struggled to express their otherworldly visions in their ephemeral art. In *The Inferno,* for instance, Dante has the Roman poet Virgil—dead a thousand years—guide him through the different levels of Hell. Present-day poets, although they have sought to address the issues of life and death in the mundane world, have not been overly discomforted by their inclination to embrace the mythic.

Finally, the Holy Bible introduces us to a veritable cornucopia of unnatural and paranormal phenomena. Within its pages are found such manifestations and intimations of an omnipotent, omniscient, and omnipresent god; flying angels; a talking snake; the resurrected dead; ghosts and apparitions; feats of magic; a virgin birth; the parting of the Red Sea; and the stopping of the sun. This is to mention but a few of the remarkable events related in the Judeo-Christian testament that proclaims the reality of an immanent power and the existence of another world.

The array of examples presented here from history and the world of painting, music, architecture, sculpture, poetry, and literature, including the Holy Bible, challenges us to acknowledge that mythic beliefs exist not only alongside rational thought—and comfortably so—but mythic fantasies and rational thought share the same mind. We are compelled, therefore, to recognize that we are at home and at one with their mutual but separate products.

Importantly, anthropological accounts attest to the universality of fables, legends, and myths. Such accounts not only support the belief that a puissant being or force intervenes in the mundane world, but they also argue for the intimate connection between the two. For instance, a Norse myth tells the story of the creation of men and women. It describes how they were the offspring of the evil frost giant, Ymir, who, while he slept, began to sweat and from the ooze under his left armpit emerged the first humans. And from East Africa there is the ironic story told by the Akamba tribe that explains how death came to be. Originally it was God's intention to endow humankind with immortality and He dispatched to Earth a chameleon to convey the good news. As it turned out, the chameleon took the assignment all too lightly and stopped on the way to Earth to catch flies. In the meantime, God changed His mind and sent a swift-flying bird to deliver His new decision that humans should be denied immortality. The bird was first to arrive and as a result humankind is condemned to die.

When we consider the occurrence of the supernatural characters or events that inhabit these myths and fables from cultures throughout the world, as well as those that are unique to Western society, we are obliged to recognize their dreamlike character. Nevertheless, we embrace such fabulations eagerly, enter into their spirit, and are enchanted—both adult and child alike.

It would appear, as Needham contends, that the mental life of society testifies to "an aspect of the imagination that is truly intrinsic to human nature" and "can be conceived as a normal, if disorderly, function of consciousness." [25]

Herbert Spencer, the nineteenth-century English sociologist and a leading exponent of a rational scientific society, did not anticipate, I am sure, that the twentieth century—with its gargantuan appetite for scientific marvels and logical discourse—would continue to embrace the paranormal or transcendental, a world that he had so zealously struggled to unseat. To the wonderment of many, the belief in a supernatural

---

[25] Needham, *Primordial Characters*, 65.

world has endured and is as alive today as it has ever been. The mass media, particularly, embraces this world as enthusiastically as it does the natural world. This can readily be seen in the films and television programs that feature angels, vampires, witches, and the other minions and familiars of both Heaven and Hell that are made even more contemporaneously authentic by the high degree of special effects and technological sophistication that is brought to their production.

A recent television recruitment commercial for the U.S. Marine Corps, for instance, features a handsome young man laboriously climbing the side of a sheer cliff. Upon reaching the top, he is confronted by a fire-breathing dragon. He alertly raises himself up to his full height, slays the beast with one thrust of a glistening silver sword, and is transformed—instantly—into a proud U.S. marine.

The fairy-tale character of this solicitation for men to go to war—to kill or be killed—provides insight into our beliefs regarding the meaning and nature of human existence. We are the inheritors of myths—myths that portray the world as a struggle: between man and man, man and beast, and good and evil. It is a world of creator and created, of mortal flesh and immortal spirit. With our dreams, visions, and fantasies, we have forged a mythic culture whose influence permeates all of life's meaningful and purposeful activities: religion, government, ethics, literature, art, civility, play, and war.

The American sociologist Peter Berger, in his challenging treatise on modern theology, *A Rumor of Angels*, was both prescient and premature when he asserted forty years ago that "the divine, at least in its classical forms, has receded into the background of human concern and consciousness."[26] Berger notes, however, that this shift from a belief system that regards

---

[26] Peter Berger, *A Rumor of Angels* (New York: Anchor Books, 1969), 5.

the transcendental as the *primum mobile* of reality to a secular worldview that maintains a scientific perspective is not without paradox. He observes that even though there is an increase in church participation, as well as in religious politics, in the United States, the motivation for such participation has radically changed. Whereas formerly people aspired to achieve religious salvation in order to avoid separation from God, Americans today participate in church life "out of a desire to provide moral instruction for their children and direction for their family life, or as part of [their] life-style."[27] The concept of a spiritual world, however, of another reality that transcends the experience of day-to-day existence and that is of ultimate significance for humankind, he contends, "is allegedly defunct or in the process of becoming defunct in the modern world."[28]

Although science, materialism, and individualism have served to undermine the role of religion in modern society, I think we should not be overly hasty in pronouncing the demise of the supernatural or its attendant sequelae. The religious impulse and its fundamental message—life after death—has neither been silenced nor vanquished. I would contend that the major reason for this resiliency is the tenacity by which individuals have continued to hold to the belief in immortality.

The Judeo-Christian creation paradigm continues to influence contemporary social life to a far greater degree than is generally recognized. While public religious rites and observances constitute the most outwardly visible expressions of the transcendental and the sacred in human life, other manifestations of its presence abound. They are found, for example, in our sexual attitudes and prohibitions, in our attitudes toward death and funeral practices, in acts of charity, in

---

[27] Berger, *A Rumor of Angels*, 2.
[28] Berger, *A Rumor of Angels*, 5.

everyday speech, and in etiquette and social display, as well as in public ceremonies and festivities, and war. It is these rarely acknowledged expressions of the transcendental vision that I now wish to address.

Before I do, permit me to discuss a concept of *culture complex*, the theoretical construct that serves as the organizing principle for the book.

Chapter 2:
Mardi Gras and the Logic of Culture

Mardi Gras, the New Orleans annual street carnival, with its deep religious roots in the Judeo-Christian creation myth, is a microcosmic expression of a *culture complex* from contemporary society. A culture complex is defined as a set of ideas, beliefs, and behaviors that function together in a purposeful and meaningful way. Although many of the facets of the complex are seemingly unrelated, they are, in fact, discrete and separate aspects of cultural life—ideas and behaviors—that come together to form a compatible and integrated whole. The beliefs and activities that are played out annually in the profane streets and sacred churches of New Orleans constitute distinct but interdependent expressions of the Christian fear of eternal damnation and separation from God. Certain aspects of the festival express a confidence in the continued survival of the New Orleans community in giving homage to the biblical command "be fruitful and multiply."

By describing Mardi Gras, which celebrates the Judeo-Christian creation myth, I will show how the different aspects of this celebration provide a microcosmic model for the manner in which certain components of our Western culture—namely, language, civility, charity, death, and the concept of the soul—serve to express and sustain the Christian belief in immortality.

At first blush, Mardi Gras strikes an observer in much the same way as our modern celebration of Halloween, that is, a contemporary reenactment of a historic folk festival, the significance of which has been diminished by time, commercialism, or license. Mardi Gras, however, is more than meets the eye. Behind the glitter, glamour, and gluttony of the festival, which has often been the primary focus of scholars in their analyses of the event, there is the profound fact of humankind's mortality and the eschatological issues surrounding mortal death. Despite its frivolous trappings and blatant commercialism, Mardi Gras dramatizes the ineffable but inextricable relationship between the flesh and the spirit. The festival dramatizes the endless quest for personal immortality as well as society's perpetual struggle to survive. An examination of this annual event will provide us with a more informed perspective concerning the issues that the festival colorfully symbolizes.

To begin, Mardi Gras is held over a period of days prior to the beginning of Lent, and is generally understood to be a time for unabashed pleasure and public merriment. Masked and gaily costumed revelers put aside the mundane nature of social life in exchange for days and nights of drunkenness, sexuality, and, not infrequently, violence. In a word, it is the "devil's workshop." It is an occasion in which law and order are suspended, and passion and self-indulgence prevail. But as we shall see, behind the glitter of costumes and the histrionics of the participants lingers the ancient quest for personal immortality and the survival of society.

Mardi Gras is sponsored by semisecret social clubs, called *krewes*, that are established along social, class, religious, and racial lines. While krewes are most often organized by neighborhoods, membership in the most prestigious krewes is, for the most part, a function of wealth and social position. The status of a krewe is reflected in the order of precedence it enjoys in the series of parades that take place over the days of the festival. The most socially prominent is the King Rex Krewe, whose parade is held on the evening of Shrove Tuesday, the day prior to Ash Wednesday—the first day of Lent.

Preparation for Mardi Gras by krewe families begins months and sometimes years before the particular parade and pageant that will feature the daughter(s) of krewe members. Mothers and aunts make forays to shopping meccas—New York, London, Rome, and Paris—in search of the wardrobes necessary for the many different occasions and functions to which the young debutantes of New Orleans society will be invited.[1]

In the meantime, the krewe organizers arrange for the purchase of thousands of dollars' worth of favors and trinkets from Italy, France, and elsewhere. These token gifts will later be tossed from the krewes' floats to the spectators at the curbside as the parade winds through Old New Orleans—Vieux Carré— to the civic auditorium. In addition to the trinkets, large truck trailers must be rented to haul the floats, a pageant planned and rehearsed, a princess and her court chosen, invitations delivered, and social engagements arranged. These are but a few of the countless details required for this annual event. These tasks are both demanding and time consuming, but of paramount importance to a participating family is the ability to pay. It has been reported that parents will bid substantial sums of money to secure their daughter(s) a place on a princess's court.[2]

A krewe's parade, like the Mardi Gras festival itself, has its own order of precedence. First to appear in the narrow, gas-lit

---

[1] Personal correspondence from Phillip Shane, New Orleans resident.
[2] Personal correspondence from Phillip Shane, New Orleans resident.

streets of Vieux Carré, are the "lumieres." These are African-American men hired for the occasion to illuminate the procession by carrying lanterns affixed to large wooden crosses. The lumieres proceed, in a sashaying manner, through the cobblestone streets while the spectators throw coins at their feet. The lumieres, without breaking step, reach down and pick up what coins they can while maintaining upright their large wooden burdens. Hard on the heels of the lumieres are the "mummers," white, adult male members of the krewe, who, masked and in white-hooded robes, ride imperiously on their Arabian stallions.[3]

Elaborately decorated floats follow the mummers. A prominent float bears the richly costumed princess of the parade and her court, who smile and wave graciously to the spectators who line the narrow streets. The following floats will carry the wives, children, and other relatives and friends of the krewe members. The occupants will toss favors, showering their largesse on the scrambling, importuning spectators. The procession eventually makes its way to the civic auditorium, where a dramatically different, but closely related, social performance unfolds.[4]

Upon arrival at the auditorium, the celebrants change into formal dress for the evening's pageant and ball. After the princess and her court and their escorts have been presented to the assemblage, they stage a theatrical presentation, following which the traditional ball begins.

After the ball, festivities are continued at private receptions. For the many young men and women who receive invitations to one or more of these social events, this series of activities will be

---

[3] Personal correspondence from Phillip Shane, New Orleans resident.

[4] Samuel Kinser, *Carnival, American Style* (University of Chicago Press: Chicago, 1990), 11.

repeated every evening until the finale—held precisely at midnight on Shrove Tuesday in the city square—when, in a dramatic climax to the preceding celebrations, the Prince of Misrule (Satan) is burned in effigy.[5]

Mardi Gras is followed by the forty-day fast of Lent, the Christian observance prior to Easter, which celebrates the resurrection of Jesus. Traditionally, penitents are expected to abstain from foods such as meat and dairy products, from entertainments and other social activities such as the celebration of marriage, and from sexual intercourse. They are expected to intensify their religious obligations and mortify themselves by performing penance, wearing hair shirts, making pilgrimages to shrines, attending religious ceremonies, and giving alms to the poor.

Mardi Gras, in its full theatrical richness, embraces two closely related but significantly different themes. First, the orgiastic festivities vividly dramatize what the world would be like if it were under Satan's rule. Superficially, it is a world of pleasure, gaiety, and excess, but beneath the pomp and glitter, it is a world awash in the seven mortal sins of pride, greed, anger, jealousy, sloth, gluttony, and lust. Ultimately, it is a world of darkness and chaos—a world that needs to be rejected if the individual, or society itself, is to survive. The Prince of Misrule (Satan) must, perforce, be killed. In the ritual burning of his effigy, New Orleans's society expresses its desire to turn away from such a world, and entreat, instead, God's mercy.

The second theme, less pronounced but nevertheless important, addresses the dual issues of the social structure of New Orleans and the ever-present challenge to its continued existence. The lavish gift-giving by the different krewes is complemented, in turn, by the spectators throwing coins at the

---

[5] Personal correspondence from Phillip Shane, New Orleans resident.

lumieres. This differential display of gift-giving serves to acknowledge the superior and inferior roles of the krewe members and the curbside spectators at the same time that it confirms and defines the subordinate role of the lumieres as being at the bottom of the social pyramid. The different krewe parades and the other social activities—both public and private—emphatically express the traditional character of New Orleans social life and the part played by class and caste in its daily affairs. [6]

The issue of the community's continuity can be observed in the courtship rituals that take place during Mardi Gras. At the invitation-only civic auditorium dances and in the private parties and family receptions that follow, the scions of New Orleans's leading families are presented and introduced to one another, with the expectation, born of tradition, that they will marry and produce the next generation of New Orleans's ruling elite.

To understand the spectacle of Mardi Gras turning suddenly from a Bacchanalian orgy into a series of religious rites and obligations, we must step back from its colorful pageantry and view the spectacle from the perspective of the Judeo-Christian *weltanschauung*. To do so permits us not only to see the connection between what is essentially street theater and the august drama of formal Easter rites played out in towering religious edifices, but it also reminds us of the sustaining power of the belief in God and the Christian quest for immortality.

Mardi Gras may thus be understood as an annual, open-air enactment of the consequences of Adam's fall. By engaging in acts of immorality and purposely overturning the good order of daily life, the participants vividly demonstrate their understanding of what the world would be without God's presence. By burning Satan's effigy and by undertaking the

---

[6] Personal correspondence from Phillip Shane, New Orleans resident.

religious duties and obligations called for during the Lenten period, the citizens of New Orleans express their contrition for their progenitor's sin as well as for their own spiritual shortcomings. By their acts of penance and oblations, they demonstrate their remorse and their fervid desire to be united with God.

In Christian culture, the mortification of the flesh has been widely practiced. Historically, the sacrifice of life itself in the name of God has been both venerated and sanctified. Penitential acts cover a wide spectrum of behaviors, including the infliction of bodily pain. Typically, such acts of mortification involve the imposition of a duty or constraint that include such acts of submission or worship as prayers, pilgrimages, tithing, sexual abstinence, dietary practices, retreats, and vows of silence. Mortification—that is, the practice of voluntarily imposing austerities upon one's body (even unto death)—has to be acknowledged as an accepted act of supplicatory behavior for Western culture.[7]

The street theater of Mardi Gras, linked inextricably as it is to the formal priestly rituals and observances of Easter, publicly declares humankind's predicament—mortal death—at the same time that it expresses its longing for its lost birthright—immortality.

Let us now turn to the different components of the *culture complex* and the varied roles they play in Western Christian culture with respect to the belief in immortality.

---

[7] Paul Thigpen, *Blood of the Martyrs, Seed of the Church* (Ann Arbor, MI: Servant, 2001).

Chapter 3:
Semen and the Soul

…it is clear both that semen possesses Soul, and that it is Soul, potentially.

—Aristotle[1]

In the Monty Python movie *The Meaning of Life*, there is a song, sung by the townspeople, that literally brings down the house. It is entitled "Every Sperm Is Sacred."

> I'm a Roman Catholic,
> And have been since before I was born,
> And the one thing they say about Catholics,
> Is they'll take you as soon as you're warm. . .
>
> You don't have to be a six-footer,
> You don't have to have a great brain,
> You don't have to have any clothes on—You're
> a Catholic the moment Dad came. . .

---

[1] Aristotle, *Generation of Animals*, IV 735a, trans. A. L. Peck (Cambridge: Harvard University Press, 1943), 155.

Because. . .

Every sperm is sacred,
Every sperm is great,
If a sperm is wasted,
God gets quite irate.

Let the heathen spill theirs,
On the dusty ground,
God shall make them pay for,
Each sperm that can't be found.

Hindu, Taoist, Mormon,
Spill theirs just anywhere,
But God loves those who treat their
Semen with more care.

Let the Pagan spill theirs,
O'er mountain, hill and plain,
God shall strike them down for
Each sperm that's spilt in vain.

The success of the film is based on its willingness to stride roughshod over one of the most proscribed Judeo-Christian taboos—the mention of the male reproductive fluid, semen. In fact this was perhaps the first instance in film history in which the word has been used—let alone made light of. As important as semen is for the propagation of the human race, racial identity, kinship, or succession, it has not been considered an acceptable subject for public discourse. Generally, reference to semen has been limited to medical literature, or more recently, to the discussion of sexual practices in the face of the AIDS pandemic.

The topic has not been completely avoided, however. The distinguished anthropologist Weston La Barre, in his book *Muelos: A Stone Age Superstition about Sexuality,* contends that human beliefs about semen constitute one of the oldest, widespread, albeit bizarre or wrongheaded (archotic), set of ideas that humankind has ever entertained.[2] According to La Barre, our early ancestors came to the erroneous conclusion that as bone is the framework of life, and semen its material vehicle, the marrow (or *muelos*) found at its center was the source of semen. The male skull, moreover, since it was believed to enclose the greatest supply of *muelos,* was the site of its most important reservoir. Eventually, both consciousness and the generative life force—semen—came to be conflated. This prehistoric conception of the source and nature of semen, La Barre contends, has been a guiding principle among peoples of the world ever since. As a result, it finds its expression in such different cultural variants as hunting rites; initiation and fertility customs; European, Asiatic, and New World head-hunting practices; Hindu religious rites (yoga); classical metaphysics; and European literature.[3]

The widespread practice of head-hunting, for example, allowed for the replenishment of the generative life force that was considered an essential, but limited, good.[4] The scalp dance of the Cheyenne Indians of North America is one such instance of this belief. Traditionally, the dance was held following a murderous raid on a neighboring village, but only when one or

---

[2] Weston La Barre, *Muelos: A Stone Age Superstition about Sexuality* (New York: Columbia University Press. 1984), 10.

[3] La Barre, *Muelos,* x.

[4] La Barre, *Muelos,* 13–14.

more heads were taken without the loss of life of a member of the raiding party. The dance served to bring together the young men and women of the tribe for the purpose of courtship and marriage. If a head were not obtained and therefore no new supply of semen acquired, the dance could not be held nor could a marriage be performed.[5]

The power attributed to semen is demonstrated as well in the buffalo dance of the Plains Indians of North America. The anthropologist Alice B. Kehoe reported on one such tribe, the Hidatsa, in which sexual intercourse was used to transfer different forms of power, political and social, as well as love and medicine. She relates that during the buffalo dance a father (an older man of the tribe) would transmit his power to a young man he desired to elevate in social status by performing sexual intercourse (actual or simulated) with the young man's wife. In effect, the young woman served as a conduit for the transfer of the power that was believed to be contained in a father's semen.[6]

Among our Western European ancestors, on the other hand, inferences regarding the historic significance of the brain stuff—semen—are based on the archeological findings from such burial sites as those at Grosse Ofnet in Bavaria, the Höhlenstein cave near Württemberg, and from Monte Circeo, Ehringsdorf, and Steinheim, Germany.[7] The evidence of forcible decapitation and the manner of burial found at these sites suggests that the practice of eating human brains in order to obtain the power, magic, or life essence of the victim reaches back at least 250,000 years. There is evidence that head-hunting was practiced in Europe well into the Bronze Age. The better-known and well-

---

[5] La Barre, *Muelos*, 14.

[6] La Barre, *Muelos*, 23.

[7] La Barre, *Muelos*, 14.

documented Celtic cult of the head, which infused much of Celtic religious tradition, has lasted down to the present but—I am pleased to report—in much less violent fashion than formerly.[8] It is seen today, vestigially, in the representation of human heads on public buildings for decorative and talismanic reasons. The familiar toast *skoal* (skull) is a relic of this tradition, a pale reminder of the life once lived by our more sanguinary ancestors.[9]

The story of the conflation of semen with the human soul is a long and complicated one. The locus of the soul in semen became authoritatively established among the classical Greeks when Aristotle declared, "It is clear both that semen possesses Soul, and that it is Soul, potentially."[10] His pronouncement has survived down through the centuries, and borne with it, as history attests, a multitude of troubles—particularly for the relationship between men and women and the status of homosexuals in society.

La Barre argues, for instance, that the tradition of Greek homosexuality, what anthropologists term "institutional homosexuality," was the ancient counterpart in Western culture to the role that semen played in Native American life. It was the tradition in certain communities of ancient Greece, La Barre reports, for a nobleman, without prejudice to his heterosexuality or his social status, to assume the responsibility of transferring to a chosen boy through social contact (including the exchange of semen) the essence of his personal qualities: his strength, sense of duty, eloquence, cleverness, generosity, courage, and other attributes. The process was not symbolic. It was a socially

---

[8] La Barre, *Muelos*, 15.

[9] La Barre, *Muelos*, 23.

[10] McKeon, Richard, ed., *The Basic Works of Aristotle: Generation of Animals*, Random House: New York, 1941, IV 735a, 30ff.

acceptable custom and considered a natural part of the lifestyle of the best men and a central factor in the education and maturation of a postpubescent boy. Through the pederastic act, as well as through intimate association with his mentor and protector, a Greek boy was initiated into manhood.[11]

The historical vigor of the belief that semen is basically located in the brain can be seen most vividly in the anatomical drawings of Leonardo da Vinci. In one sagittal section of his male illustrations, da Vinci drew ducts (that do not exist) that purportedly served to convey semen from the cerebrospinal canal to the male genital. It is interesting to note, moreover, that da Vinci's anatomical drawings were not withdrawn from Italian medical texts for another 200 years.[12]

The material world, La Barre contends, can be taken for granted; it just is. It is birth and death that are the mysteries that we humans must confront. Clearly, the presence of life is associated with breath, what the Greeks called *pneuma.* The force that animates life, though never seen, they called the *anima,* or what we now call the soul. It was conceived as imperishable and separate from the physical human body. The belief in the anima served to explain to the ancients the persistent patterning that is found in all living things and was recognized as that which vitalized the endless cycle of birth and rebirth. This mysterious patterning, which La Barre calls "an immortal logos-pattern," came to be viewed as the male principle because it was believed that only through the male was life possible. Essentially, the male principle, metaphorically, was perceived as the masculine template that impressed itself upon the formless feminine substance. As La Barre states, our early ancestors:

---

[11] La Barre, *Muelos,* 79.
[12] La Barre, *Muelos,* 3.

> ...viewed the growth of a child in a woman's body as no mystery. The increment comes from the food the mother eats, quite as later growth comes from the milk she gives her child. The mystery lies in the inception of life: consciousness, life, warmth that appears to be a male gift and surely from his semen.[13]

In this light, it should be observed that the perception of a woman as simply a vessel through which men are born is not limited solely to their role in childbirth. What is at stake here is much greater than simply the issue of who contributes most, if not all, to the life of a child. The essential issue that these ideas raise is: What is the basic nature of women? Are women materially and psychologically the same as men? It is not the patronizing question Freud once raised: "What do women want?" Rather, it is the more biologically and psychologically relevant question: "What are they?" Do they live on the same moral, physical, or intellectual plane as men? Our Greek forbearers replied to that question with a resounding "no," much to the detriment of Greek women, as well as to women in general in modern Western culture. The ancient Greeks believed that women were "failed men."[14] This idea, propounded by Aristotle, following Plato, taught that men of the first generation of humans who were cowardly or lived immoral lives where reborn as women and, as a result, were accorded a secondary role in Greek society, subsequently to be "categorized alongside children, foreigners and slaves."[15] The profoundly deleterious consequences of this idea—that women are a lesser order of

---

[13] La Barre, *Muelos*, 2.

[14] La Barre, *Muelos*, 73.

[15] Morag Buchan, *Women in Plato's Political Theory* (New York: Routledge, 1999), 41.

human being (emotional and earthbound) and consequently possess inferior souls that deny them the ability to embrace philosophy or higher reason—has resonated throughout the Western world down to the present. I am reminded of the recent contretemps between the president of Harvard University and his faculty when they interpreted his remarks to imply that women may indeed still suffer from this Aristotelian canard . He was ultimately obliged to resign his office. One can only speculate how different things might be between men and women today if Aristotle had insisted that one's soul appeared in the temporal world—male and female alike—with one's mother's milk.

One aspect of the belief in the immortality of the soul and its identification with the male is primogeniture, the historic practice whereby the eldest son inherits all, or a disproportionate share, of his father's estate.[16] The intent behind the tradition was understood to be the orderly transfer of property and other goods and chattel from one generation to another. More recently, however, archeological discoveries at Ugarit, Syria, suggest that the practice also served to provide the firstborn son with the resources and wherewithal to offer prayers and perform sacrifices on behalf of his deceased father's soul.[17]

Implicit in the practice of primogeniture is the belief that praise and sacrifice to God, endlessly repeated throughout the generations of fathers and sons, secured the survival of the deceased's soul. While primogeniture is no longer practiced in most Western societies today as a principle of inheritance, it continues nevertheless to be the basis of succession for the royal

---

[16] Laurence Perceval, *Law and Custom of Primogeniture* (Cambridge: J. Hall & Son, 1878, Sect. I), 1–25.

[17] Theodore J. Lewis, *Cults of the Dead in Ancient Israel and Ugarit* (Otterup: Scholars Press, 1989), 53.

house of England and certain other royal and aristocratic families of Europe, including the Grimaldi family of the principality of Monaco.[18]

The Ugarit discoveries suggest that continued contact between the living and the dead in those ancient times was accepted within the normal course of events. The researchers report that it was the practice for a pipe to be inserted into the family tomb, which was typically located beneath the floor of the deceased's house, in order to allow food and water to be passed directly into it.[19] The firstborn son was designated, according to the Ugarit text, as his father's "caretaker," "water-pourer," and "name caller."[20]

The Sumerian epic *Gilgamesh* provides us with additional insight into the importance attributed to the male heir in antiquity and the fate of his father's soul. It is poignantly illustrated in a conversation that Gilgamesh had with the spirit of Enkidu, his former companion and alter ego, who is confined to Hell. Gilgamesh inquires of Enkidu's spirit: "Have you seen the man who has no son?" The spirit responds,

> "I have seen him. He..." [response broken off]
> "The one with one son: have you seen him?"
> "I have seen him.

---

[18] "Primogeniture" 2005 Encyclopaedia Britannica on-line. Dec. 2005 <http://www.britannica.com/ebc/article-9375896?query=primogeniture&ct=> It's of interest to note that the treaty of 1918 between France and the sovereign principality of Monaco specifies that in the event the Grimaldi dynasty (founded in 1297) failed to produce a male heir, the citizens of Monaco would lose their unique identity as well as their exemption from taxation and military service.

[19] Lewis, *Cults of the Dead*, 172.

[20] Marvin H. Pope, "The Cult of the Dead at Ugarit," in *Ugarit in Retrospect*, ed. Gordon D. Young (Winona Lake, IN: Eisenbrauns, 1982) 159.

He lies under the wall, weeping bitterly."
"The one with two sons: have you seen him?"
"I have.
"He lives in a brick house and eats bread."
"The one with three sons: have you seen him?"
"I have."
He drinks water out of waterskins filled from
deep wells."
"The one with four sons: have you seen him?"
"I have.
His heart rejoices."
"The one with five sons: have you seen him?
"I have.
Like a good writer, scribe to a king, his hand is
revealed.
He brings justice to the palace."
"The one with six sons: have you seen him?"
"I have.
Like the man who guides the plow, he feels
pride."
"The one with seven sons: have you seen him?"
"I have.
Like a man close to the gods."[21]

The text is broken off for the man "who had no son," but given the development of the narrative, it is implicit that his is the worst of fates. He was bereft; he died without benefit of a son who would be expected—indeed, obligated—to conduct his funeral, attend to his tomb, protect his name, and honor his memory. Five thousand years ago, a man who died leaving seven sons to survive him enjoyed a "blessed state," even in death.

---

[21] Gilgamesh, trans and ed. John Gardner and John Maier (New York: Vintage Books, 1985), 265.

The recent archeological discovery at Ugarit also helps to illuminate the biblical story of Isaac and his two sons, Jacob and Esau, in their struggle to obtain Isaac's blessing. What was at stake in this filial contest was not only the blessing and all that it entailed to the earthly benefit of the recipient but also the right and obligation to perform the funeral duties and sacrifices associated with Isaac's death and memorialization that would redound, spiritually, to the performer's credit. This priestly role is important for not only understanding the historic practice of primogeniture but also its signal importance in the quest for one's immortality.

The concept of primogeniture calls forth still another series of related practices and observances associated with the singularly important question of birth that also finds its rationale in the Judeo-Christian paradigm. Laws concerning adultery, for instance, find their basis in the requirement that the firstborn son is the legitimate and true biological heir of the father. The potency of the firstborn son's oblations as funeral priest, consequently, rests upon his mother's sexual purity. In this light, the proscription against adultery and the severe penalties attached to it—especially for the offending wife—becomes clear. That is, a wife's adultery involves much more than the violation of her marriage vows or the infliction of emotional or proprietary injury upon the offended husband. Simply put, the fate of the husband's soul is at spiritual risk and the prospect of his immortality jeopardized if the male child is not of his issue.

The importance of the practice of primogeniture is illustrated in the case of Onan whom, we are informed in the Book of Genesis (38:9–10), God struck dead because he refused to impregnate his dead brother's childless widow, choosing instead to "spill his seed on the ground." Such severe punishment can only be understood with the recognition of the spiritually critical role of the firstborn son. Under the ancient Hebrew custom of the levirate, a surviving brother was expected, indeed, in some instances, obliged by law, to provide the dead brother with a son to serve him as a funeral priest.[22] Although today the meaning of the word *onanism* is more commonly understood as a euphemism for the practice of masturbation, biblically its meaning was far more dire——it meant to place in spiritual jeopardy a dead brother's soul. But a caveat is in order. Pope Pius XI, in his 1930 encyclical *Casti Cannubii,* accepts the modern interpretation, that is, it was the pope's view that Onan was killed for practicing what the church terms "sterile lust." The encyclical states:

> Wherefore it is not surprising that the Sacred Scriptures themselves also bear witness to the fact that the divine Majesty attends this unspeakable depravity [masturbation] with the utmost detestation, sometimes having punished it with death, as St. Augustine recalls: 'For it is illicit and shameful for a man to lie with even his lawful wife in such a way as to prevent the conception of offspring. This is what, Onan son of Judah, used to do; and for that God slew him.'[23]

I suspect, however, if that were God's sole objection to Onan's behavior, then scarce one pubescent boy out of ten thousand would survive His wrath.

The historic prescription that a woman be a virgin at the time of her marriage is not restricted to Western culture. In Japan, for instance, the empress is still described today in official court documents as the "perfect vessel." Such a designation reflects

---

[22] Philip W. Goetz, "Levirate," *The New Encyclopaedia Britannica*, 179.

[23] "Casti Cannubii," *Encyclical of Pope Pius XI on Christian Marriage*, Article 55, 1930.

the elaborate precautions that are traditionally taken to ensure that the emperor's consort is a virgin at the time of her marriage. The more highly publicized instance of this practice that is still observed within the Western world is, of course, the case of Princess Diana of England who, before her marriage to Prince Charles, was obliged to submit to just such an examination.[24]

Such conscientious surveillance regarding a woman's chastity historically dates back to the Book of Deuteronomy (22:13–18), where tokens of a woman's virginity were put on public display. To this day in different Mediterranean countries—Italy, for example—it continues to be the custom for a family to display the sheet from their daughter's conjugal bed in order to demonstrate that she had been chaste at the time of her marriage. (It has been reported by more than one wag, however, that this practice over the centuries has cost the lives of an untold number of chickens.)

Paralleling these practices and proscriptions that speak to the issues of adultery, masturbation, and chastity are found other prohibitions that serve to make up the culture-complex as it relates to sexual behavior in the Judeo-Christian paradigm— namely, the historic ban against incest, homosexuality, prostitution, and bestiality.

In Leviticus, for example, we read, "You must not uncover the nakedness of your father or mother," "You must not uncover the nakedness of your sister," "You must not uncover the nakedness of the daughter of your son or daughter," "You must not uncover the nakedness of your mother's sister," "You must not uncover the nakedness of your daughter-in-law," "You

---

[24] "Betrothal of Camila," *Daily Star*, February 2006, available at http://64.233.179.104/search?q=cache:S4Ne7t6D_lsJ:www.thedailystar.n et/2005/03/18/d50318110595.htm+%22virginity+test%22+%22princes s+diana%22&hl=en&gl=us&ct=clnk&cd=7.

must not uncover the nakedness of your brother's wife,"[25] "If a man lies with a male as with a woman, both of them have committed an abomination: they shall be put to death,"[26] "The man who lies with an animal: he must die,"[27] and "Do not profane your daughter by making her a prostitute."[28]

Within the Judeo-Christian canon, such behavior is judged as an affront to God and a rejection of his gift of life. It is a grievous moral fault. God is blasphemed when a man commits such sterile acts because the sacred seed of life—semen—is dishonored, even as it is dissipated.

With the conflation of semen and soul, the role of the male became paramount in death as well as in life. Primogeniture became the rule whereby a firstborn son was required to perform the sacerdotal rites and oblations that ensured the survival of his father's soul. With this concept, however, came another set of ideas that expanded with the rise of Christianity into what was to become a burdensome set of issues—namely, the humiliation and denigration of women in Western society and the militant repudiation of homosexuality.

As the father's funeral priest, the religious efficacy of the son's ministrations depended on the sexual purity of his mother. Consequently, since biblical times she has had to submit to a proof of her virginity.

But the concern regarding the survival of the soul after death, resting as it did on the sexual purity of the mother, brought forth laws concerning adultery and other customs and observances having to do with human sexuality.

---

[25] The Holy Bible: Revised Standard Version, (New York: Thomas Nelson & Sons, 1946), Leviticus 18:7, 10, 13, 15, 16.

[26] Leviticus 19:29

[27] Leviticus 20:15.

[28] Leviticus 19:29.

Semen, as the material vehicle of the soul, is sacred. Its profanation by such acts as homosexuality, bestiality, incest, adultery, and masturbation, viewed as "sterile lust," has long been proscribed by Western society.

The idea of the soul and the belief that its telic purpose is to be reunited with the divine is one of humankind's most generative visions and the foundation of much of what we have come to recognize as Western culture. The idea of the soul and its historic identification with the male brings with it the diminishment of the status of women in such aspects of life as the right to control one's body, to perform religious sacraments, to own property, or to represent oneself in court, to cite but a few of the indignities and humiliations that the female has had to suffer and endure. So, too, in the realm of sexual behavior, the long-term struggle to accept homosexual behavior speaks to the demeaning and destructive legacy that the idea of the soul and its conflation with semen has left us.

Chapter 4: Language

Sticks and stones may break my bones
But words can never hurt me.

—Childhood adage

According to the Judeo-Christian account of creation, the utterances of God formed heaven and earth, while Adam, His first human creation, was given the privilege of naming all of the other creatures.[1] To speak, therefore, is a profoundly puissant act that is viewed as one of God's greatest gifts to humankind.

What God gives, however, God can also take away. This is illustrated in compelling fashion by the biblical account of the Tower of Babel. Fearful that humans would become like Himself—that is, immortal—God confounded their speech, causing the different peoples of the world to be unable to communicate with one another.[2] This act, which led to the scattering of people throughout the world, not only reminds us of the importance of language but also underscores the

---

[1] Genesis 1:18.
[2] Genesis 11:1–9.

vulnerability of humankind and the daunting challenge confronting them in their historic quest for immortality.

Historical accounts give abundant evidence for humankind's respect for the word, as well as for the word-crafter. Since before the time of our Greek ancestors, the poet, the orator, and the singer possessed one thing that was held to be of inestimable value—command of the word. According to the historian Onians, Greek heroes found immortality through the recitation and singing of their accomplishments by their companions-in-arms.[3]

The consequence of God's action of depriving humankind of a common language to frustrate their desire for immortality has resonated to the present. With the estrangement of the human community, other divisive consequences followed, including the practice of cryptography (secret writing) in which humans, taking a page out of God's own book, sought to confuse one another even further by means of graphic legerdemain. The Hebrew encoding system, the *atbash*, for instance, almost as old as the Tower of Babel itself, bespeaks of God's creature who learned well the lesson: to confound is to conquer.[4]

Language's ability to divide or mystify applies not only to cryptology or to the many different languages that now co-exist in the world; it can also apply to a single language. The popular musical play *My Fair Lady* specifically addresses this issue. The play demonstrates (with wit and humor) how the English language functions to separate and distinguish one individual from another in social intercourse. It effectively illustrates how words can identify the rich from the poor, the educated from the ignorant, and the young from the old. Furthermore, the play illustrates how the structure of social life is not only expressed

---

[3] Jaeger, "The Greek Ideas of Immortality," 137.
[4] David Kahn, *The Code Breakers* (New York: Scribner, 1996), chap. 3.

through certain linguistic forms but also how the forms serve to support it. The importance of language, it cannot be gainsaid, reaches far beyond the single function of enabling one person to communicate with another. It is a countervailing force that can lead to misunderstanding, mystification, and ultimately, as with the Trappist order of monks, to compulsory silence. As it has been observed, "language is no mere instrument that we can control at will; it controls us."[5]

Tradition has it that the spoken word in specific contexts is immutable. In connection with the earlier discussion regarding birthright, Isaac mistakenly blessed Jacob instead of his firstborn son, Esau. The narrative tells us that despite acknowledging his mistake, Isaac could not rescind the blessing once it had been given—the belief in the irrevocable nature of the spoken word prevented him from doing so.[6]

Perhaps the most fateful words spoken in recent history that were never rescinded were uttered by Kaiser Wilhelm II of Germany prior to the First World War. He promised Franz Joseph, the emperor of Austria-Hungary, that he could rely on Germany's "faithful support" in the event that the punitive action the emperor planned against Serbia would bring Austria-Hungary into conflict with Russia.[7] This promise was in response to the assassination of the Austrian crown prince, Franz Ferdinand, on June 28, 1914, by a Serbian national that ultimately led to the outbreak of the war. According to the political scientist John Stoessinger in his book *Why Nations go to War*, the kaiser's pledge was of the order of a *Nibelungentreue*, a blood oath that is both sacred and irrevocable. The kaiser's

---

[5] David Mellinkoff, *The Language of the Law* (Boston: Little Brown, 1990), vii.

[6] Genesis 27:37.

[7] John G. Stoessinger, *Why Nations Go to War*, 6th ed. (New York: St. Martins Press, 1993), 3–4.

conflation of personal ethics with political judgment led to the most calamitous war in human history up to that time.[8]

The immutability of the word can also be observed in the practice of law. When a bill of particulars is presented concerning a crime or felony, its wording must in every way reflect the true facts of the case before the court. It must conform to what Mellinkoff describes as "the dogma of precision," or it will be declared null and void, and the charges against the accused dismissed. This rule not only embraces the substantive issues of the case but can also include such secondary particulars as the time or place of the offense or the means employed.[9]

Language, we have come to learn, serves to illuminate the hierarchical structure of society through its particular usage. The power and persistence of language's association with the sacred and the transcendental is seen in the role that Latin continues to play in the contemporary world. Just as we conduct everyday affairs in what is termed standard or vernacular English, we conduct certain activities (albeit, often limited to the written word) in Latin, specifically in professions having to do with God's authority (law), His divinity (theology), or His beneficence (medicine). Latin is the spoken language of the Christian God and through it His authority over all life is made manifest. Above the entrance to Columbia University Medical School in New York City is the inscription, in Latin, "From the Highest Cometh Healing," proclaiming to one and all that doctors are essentially the hand servants of God.

It is also seen in the Adamic tradition of giving all forms of life a proper name (in Latin) including humankind itself—*Homo sapiens.*

---

[8] Stoessinger, *Why Nations Go to War,* 4
[9] Mellinkoff, *The Language of the Law,* 387.

Language identifies an activity at the same time that it sets it apart. The romance languages—French, Spanish and Italian—together with their omnipresent progenitor, Latin, not only inform us of the nature of the activity that is occurring, but these languages also serve to confirm the activity's value as well as the social status of the participants. Again, the musical play *My Fair Lady* illustrates this point in an entertaining fashion: diction and dialect—not dialogue—denote the lady.

Even the manner of how one forms the written word contains a subtle statement about a man's or woman's status in society. Exclusive private schools will employ a script that readily distinguishes their students from those who attend a public school. While the public school script that is taught is typically Italianate or cursive, the style of writing promoted in private schools is often of a contrary style, perpendicular or grave. Penmanship, like a pair of bespoken shoes, makes the man.

While immigration from different corners of the world has swelled the American population considerably over the past few decades and introduced the nation to a mélange of languages on a scale perhaps never before experienced, vernacular English remains the *lingua franca* of the United States. American society, nevertheless, associates different languages with different social activities, in keeping with the class and occupational distinctions that exist. One need only look at the printed menu for an official dinner at the White House or at some other august occasion, for instance, to see that French—not English—is the preferred language when it comes to formal dining. The *haute monde* will have its *haute cuisine*.

So, too, in music is this same practice found. Musical notation is traditionally in the Italian language, regardless of the linguistic or ethnic background of a musician. It is Italian that sets the tone of musical instruction.

Philologists and social scientists have long commented on the fact that certain words, while familiar, are nevertheless unutterable. As a subset of the language, swearing or cursing is not a simple act of speech. One does not simply open one's mouth and ejaculate sounds that others find rude or offensive. Swearing involves a complex system of meanings and understandings. To swear an oath on the Bible, for example, is socially approved while to utter a curse or an obscenity is met with censure.

The so-called four-letter words that are considered obscene are not indiscriminately scattered about the language but are words perceived to be, essentially, of Anglo-Saxon origin, even though some are not.[10] Anglo-Saxon, the vestigial speech of the early Britons, is today the language of the street (and gutter) and must continue to bear not only the historical shame of defeat in battle (the Normans invaded England in 1066 CE) but must also carry the burden of identifying what is held to be corrupt in the Western Christian world, namely, the human body. Nowhere is the distinction between body and soul more clearly demonstrated than in the obscenities uttered by the heirs to the Christian tradition to those whom they would insult. Anglo-Saxon must endure alone the offensive deprecatory vulgarisms: shit, fart, cock, cunt, and fuck.

These obscenities, by implication, characterize the human body as the source of what is foul and disgusting in human life and give testimony to the body's corruptibility and mortality. The body, we have come to learn, is an impediment to our quest for immortality. When an obscenity is uttered, therefore, one is expressing disgust for the human body at the same time that the person to whom the vulgarism is addressed is, by association, vilified. In doing so, the speaker disassociates himself or herself

---

[10] Richard Dooling, *Blue Streak* (New York: Random House, 1996), 32.

from the corruptible body, disavows it, and by implication declares his or her spiritual affinity with the soul.

We see this attitude toward the body expressed to this day, not only in cursing but also when we offer our right hand in greeting. To offer one's left hand is considered an insult, as the left hand is seen as spiritually unclean. The expression, "a left-handed compliment," therefore, reflects this attitude and rather than being a compliment is, to the contrary, an insult. In politics, we find the same negativity associated with the left. The party of the left is associated with labor and the landless, while the party designated as the right suggests the possession of property and political conservatism. This distinction is also seen when one expresses the hope or expectation that one day he or she may sit at the right hand of God.[11]

In the singular quest to overcome death and be reunited with God, the Judeo-Christian community has attempted to placate Him, mitigate His judgment, and win His favor. With the employment of Latin, for instance, we claim a close affinity to His principles and purposes not only within the sacerdotal office but without. Additionally, in keeping with His will, we accept the immutability and puissance of the word. Moreover, our social institutions, such as the church and the state, are both defined and described in the language of God. By the use of this sacerdotal tongue, we are both comforted in our belief in God's mercy and reassured that our spiritual aspirations to be reunited with Him will be realized.

---

[11] Robert Hertz, *The Pre-Eminence of the Right Hand: A Study in Religious Polarity in Death and the Right Hand*, trans. by Rodney Needham and Claudia Needham (Glencoe, IL: Free Press, 1960), 89–174.

Chapter 5:
Civility

Laura Thornburgh, a sometime leading arbiter of good manners, informs us that the basic principle underlying etiquette, or a code of social conduct, is altruism, the concern for the well-being or rights of another.[1] As human beings assemble to worship, eat, exchange goods, celebrate, or bury the dead, common sense and good order require standards of behavior, the absence of which might not only lead to much confusion or conflict but also defeat the purpose of the gathering itself. History is in no small part a record of the establishment of codes of conduct, whether they relate to worship, kingship, citizenship, kinship, or friendship.

The history of such codes is ancient. Even before the Mosaic Code was revealed (circa 1300 BCE), the Code of Hammurabi detailed the rights, privileges, and duties of both king and citizens and is recognized as the first major charter extant to establish the rules of social behavior.[2] The code consists of the legal decisions made during the reign of Hammurabi (1792–

---

[1] Laura Thornburgh, *Etiquette for Everybody* (New York: Barse, 1923), vi.
[2] *Encyclopaedia Britannica, Micropaedia*, 878.

1750 BCE) of the first Babylonian dynasty. It was inscribed on a diorite stele and placed in the temple of Marduk, the national god. The laws inscribed on the stele provided for rules of trade (prices and tariffs), family contracts (marriage and divorce), and laws covering criminal (assault, theft) and civil issues (slavery, debt). Penalties varied according to the status of the offender and the circumstances of the offense.

The background of the code is a body of Sumerian law but the text is in the Akkadian (Semitic) language. The code was meant to be applied to a wider realm than any single country and to integrate Semitic and Sumerian traditions and peoples. Moreover, despite a few primitive survivals relating to family solidarity, trial by ordeal, and the *lex talionis* (i.e., an eye for an eye, a tooth for a tooth), the code was advanced far beyond tribal custom and recognized no blood feud, private retribution, or marriage by capture.[3]

The Rosetta stone of Egypt, the Mosaic laws of the Israelites, the Magna Carta of England, and the Constitution of the United States each, in its own way, echoes the Code of Hammurabi, while each expresses the particular aspirations of its respective society. Taken together, though separated by thousands of years and representing the unique visions of five singular cultures, they share the same general goals regarding humankind's desire for law and order. Simply put, the different charters ascribe to a world created by a god or gods: a world under the authority of an ineffable creator to whom we owe our individual lives and, indeed, existence itself. This authority is represented on Earth by figures of lesser power—kings, priests, and governmental officials—who, in turn, are entitled to their own degree of honor and respect. Citizens are charged to maintain the good

---

[3] *Encyclopaedia Britannica, Micropaedia,* 878.

order and well-being of society through responsible civic behavior.

Norbert Elias, the noted European social historian, describes in his book *The History of Manners* the signal landmarks that he terms *civilité* in the historical process.[4] His analysis of the development of personal conduct has helped to illuminate the many different changes in the manner of one's personal behavior that have occurred over the centuries in Western society. His book traces these refinements in personal deportment that transpired from the Middle Ages to the nineteenth century and addresses such issues as the manner of one's speech, table etiquette, natural bodily functions, aggression, and gender-based relationships. It is his conclusion that socially undesirable impulses or idiosyncratic behavior has been generally discouraged or repressed over the centuries, while what has been considered refined, delicate, or hygienic has been generally promoted, if not specifically prescribed.[5]

In the early part of the sixteenth century, following the challenge to the Catholic Church by the reform-minded priest Martin Luther, dramatic changes were in the air. Apart from the profound changes that the Protestant Reformation effected in religious belief and behavior, it served to revolutionize the social conduct of men and women and the behavior of children.

Led by such religious zealots as Luther (1483–1546), Calvin (1509–1564), and Knox (1510–1572), the Protestant upheaval placed the burden of salvation squarely on the shoulders of an individual with the theological clarion call: by faith alone. As a consequence, one's personal conduct came to be seen as under the direct scrutiny of God. Heretofore, the Catholic Church,

---

[4] Norbert Elias, *The History of Manners* (New York: Pantheon Books, 1978), chap. 1.

[5] Elias, *The History of Manners*, 150.

through its priestly functionaries, was the sole arbiter of an individual's fate and the church's intercession was deemed essential for salvation. Bertrand Russell, in his *A History of Western Philosophy,* observed that a Catholic priest literally held the keys to the Kingdom of Heaven. He explained:

> The clergy possessed certain miraculous powers, especially in connection with the sacraments…without the help of the clergy, marriage, absolution, and extreme unction were impossible. Even more important…only a priest could perform the miracle of the mass.
>
> Owing to their miraculous powers, priests could determine whether a man should spend eternity in heaven or in hell. If he died while excommunicate, he went to hell; if he died after the priest performed all the proper ceremonies, he would ultimately go to heaven provided he had duly repented and confessed. Before going to heaven, however, he would have to spend some time—perhaps a very long time—suffering the pains of purgatory.
>
> All of this, it must be understood, was genuinely and firmly believed both by priests and by laity; it was not merely a creed officially professed.[6]

By dismissing the priesthood's critical role of arbiter and intermediary, the newfound convert to Protestantism found himself or herself naked before God's judgment and personally obliged to confront—alone—not only the ontological issue of mortality but also the eschatological issue of immortality.

---

[6] Bertrand Russell, *The History of Philosophy* (New York: Simon and Schuster, 1945), 408.

Without the historical support of the Church and having to manage one's life as well as negotiate one's salvation, the Protestant convert turned to the plethora of books that provided instructions on personal conduct. Erasmus of Rotterdam (ca. 1469–1536), the most prominent philosopher of the age, published a short treatise, *De Civilitate Morum Puerilium* (*On the Civility of Children,* circa 1530) that immediately achieved an unprecedented circulation. According to Elias, in the first six years after the book's publication, it was reprinted more than thirty times and by end of the eighteenth century more than 130 editions of the book appeared in such different languages as German, Czech, French, and English.[7] Other guides for correct social behavior soon followed and there appeared an etiquette literature that also called for spiritual submission and conformity in thought and behavior.[8]

I would contend that this advocacy of civility and good manners was more than just an expression of altruism or concern for the other, as Thornburgh assumes, but rather it had an important theological subscript—do nothing that might offend God. This concern for the correct relationship between oneself and God was significantly enhanced by the Protestant Reformation and by the new lay priest that it produced.

Let us consider, for example, the religious concepts that serve to underpin the rules and observances that govern eating rituals and activities: the recognition of a creator; the mortification of the body; the distinction between the symbolically pure right hand and the unclean left; and the distinction between the sacred and profane. These religious categories are strictly observed in the course of the seemingly simple act of sharing a meal. In this light we can understand

---

[7] Elias, *The History of Manners*, 54.
[8] Elias, *The History of Manners*, 79.

more clearly the formal rites of the table and its proscriptive etiquette that has been rigorously observed throughout the Western world for centuries.

Thornburgh instructs us that the proper etiquette of formal dining begins with a prayer of thanks to God: "Bless us, O Lord, and these Thy gifts, which we are about to receive from Thy bounty, through Christ our Lord. Amen."

The mortification or disciplining of the body is seen in such rules as sitting straight, prohibiting elbows on the table, requiring one's hands to be on the lap when not eating, and avoiding touching the face or twisting or touching the hair. It is seen as well in the extended time and effort generally expended in learning the formal rules of dining.

The religious distinction between the right hand and the left is seen most clearly in the custom of seating a guest of honor on the right hand of the host. Water goblets and wine glasses are also served from the right in recognition of their association with the sacramental whereas food is always served from the left in keeping with the Christian view of the body as profane.

It should be noted that Thornburgh does not discuss the taboo subject of flatulence or other natural functions of the body in a public setting. In a world that searches for spiritual approval and ways to be closer to God, the mention of such normal functions of the profane and corrupt human body is beyond the pale.

The religious imperative can be observed in other areas of social life as well, but perhaps not always with the same degree of clarity. Its recognition, however, can help us understand better, for instance, the motivation for the ostentatious behavior of the American social elite that the celebrated American economist Thorsten Veblen identified in the latter half of the nineteenth century: behavior he sardonically labeled "conspicuous consumption." In his classic book *The Theory of the*

Leisure Class, Veblen decried such behavior as the construction of ostentatious homes, the profligate use of space and time, the tireless pursuit of nonutilitarian activities, frivolous entertainments, and the relentless quest in search of what is unique or rare as a flagrant waste of the Earth's and the communities' finite resources.[9]

To be understood, Veblen must be located—like Marx and Freud—within his time, a time of scientific materialism. For him, the measure of man was man, and the creation of society was solely a human accomplishment. The challenge of life was one of survival—as much for society as for the individual. Essentially, it meant that economic behavior was the critical activity that scholars needed to examine if one were to understand the basic dynamics of society. Social utility was the byword. But herein can be found the Achilles' heel in Veblen's otherwise brilliant analysis of American social institutions. As a self-professed atheist who publicly expressed his dubious regard for the Judeo-Christian paradigm, Veblen did not appreciate the singular importance of religious faith in American social life.[10] The German sociologist Max Weber, on the other hand, understood more clearly the underlying influence of the religious legacy in the economic life of a country. In his classic treatise *Protestantism and the Spirit of Capitalism*, Weber argued that the religious teachings of Protestantism—particularly those of Calvin and his followers—profoundly influenced the way in which his adherents understood not only the meaning of life

---

[9] Thorsten Veblen, *The Theory of the Leisure Class* (New York: Penguin Books, 1983).

[10] Joseph Dorfman, *Thorsten Veblen and His America* (New York: Augustus M. Kelley, 1966).

and work but also came to re-interpret—in the light of their stringent religious beliefs—the possession of great wealth.[11]

It needs to be recalled that in Genesis, God said to Adam: "cursed is the ground because of you, in toil you shall eat of it all the days of your life. In the sweat of your face you shall eat bread till you return to the ground, for out of it you were taken, you are dust, and to dust you shall return."[12]

Hard, unremitting work, therefore, was demanded by the Calvinists and seen as their just burden.

Over time, however, the United States prospered. The efforts of different individuals led to unprecedented commercial and industrial success. With this success came the acquisition of great wealth. There emerged the idea, Weber contends, that such wealth constituted a sign that God had mitigated His judgment for a chosen few. These fortunate ones, therefore, persuaded themselves to believe that they could possibly look forward to a life after death and reunion with God.

In this light, what Veblen failed to perceive were the underlying religious convictions that guided and orchestrated the behavior of the American Protestant elite that he so delighted in castigating. It must be remembered that the Bible instructs the faithful "to live as the birds of the air and the lilies of the field and to give no thought for the morrow."[13] Such biblical assurances of God's benevolence made it possible for the newly rich Americans to revel in their good fortune and to demonstrate to all the world by the inordinate display of their wealth not only their faith in the limitless beneficence of God but also their exclusive membership among the religious elect.

---

[11] Max Weber, *The Protestant Ethic and the Rise of Capitalism* (New York: Charles Scribner's Sons, 1958).

[12] Genesis 3:17–19.

[13] Matthew 6:25–34.

The counterpoint to this behavior is, of course, the much-maligned and caricatured figure of the miser in Western culture. At first blush, he is seen as someone who is cheap, stingy, or worse, selfish. We often seek an explanation for such behavior, attributing it to a personality disorder or perhaps to someone who has experienced extremely difficult times, such as those who lived through the Great Depression of the 1930s. From a religious perspective, however, such a person can be seen as one who is lacking in faith, one who does not trust in Christ's promise. It is this distrust, I would argue, that has been historically censured. Evidence of this point of view can be seen in the religiously inspired rebuke that emanated from American Protestant pulpits during Veblen's time by clergy, throughout the country, who decried the promotion of personal life insurance as expressing a lack of faith in God's beneficence.[14]

History records the human desire for fame and glory and the sociobiologist would insist that colorful and flamboyant display in the animal/human world has genetic roots in the mating instinct. But I would agree with Weber that the conspicuous consumption of the American Protestant elite that Veblen deplored with such acerbic skill found a significant measure of its motivation in the conviction of their faith and their fervent belief in their deliverance from mortal death.

Ours is a hierarchical world. We ascribe the creation of the world to God or to an ineffable creator to whom we owe our existence. History, moreover, records from earliest times humankind's search for law and order in keeping with the presumed will of the creator. The accepted establishment of Earthly authority—king, government official, judge, and

---

[14] Viviana A. Rotman Zelizer, *Morals and Markets: The Development of Life Insurance in the United States* (New Brunswick, NJ: Transaction Books, 1983), 73.

priest—reflects these aspirations. The role of the priest, particularly in his capacity as the Earthly adjudicator and possessor of the efficacious rites and rituals critical to the fate of a parishioner's soul, played a primary role in the life of the Christian community. The Protestant Reformation, under Martin Luther, radically changed that relationship and subsequently obliged the Protestant supplicant—following the shibboleth "faith alone"—to negotiate his salvation on his own. Books on manners and table etiquette soon followed as the newly dispossessed Protestants struggled to discover the proper mode of behavior that would find favor in the eyes of a judgmental god. The conspicuous consumption of the nineteenth-century heirs to the Protestant upheaval of the sixteenth century is testimony to the belief that they had found that favor.

Chapter 6:
Charity

Good King Wenceslas looked out
On the feast of Stephen
When the snow lay round about
Deep and crisp and even
Brightly shone the moon that night
Though the frost was cruel
When a poor man came in sight
Gath'ring winter fuel

"Hither, page, and stand by me
If thou know'st it, telling
Yonder peasant, who is he?
Where and what his dwelling?"
"Sire, he lives a good league hence
Underneath the mountain
Right against the forest fence
By Saint Agnes' fountain."

"Bring me flesh and bring me wine
Bring me pine logs hither

Thou and I will see him dine
When we bear him thither."
Page and monarch forth they went
Forth they went together
Through the rude wind's wild lament
And the bitter weather

"In his master's steps he trod
Where the snow lay dinted
Heat was in the very sod
Which the Saint had printed
Therefore, Christian men, be sure
Wealth or rank possessing
Ye who now will bless the poor
Shall yourselves find blessing

—John Mason Neale, 1853

The charitable impulse to render assistance to another—friend or stranger—finds its inspiration in the belief of a benign and loving God and the conviction that human equality is intrinsic to our divinely inspired existence: all persons are equal; all are brothers; all are children of God.[1] This idea was made tangible by the efforts of the Old Testament Israelites to provide for their fellow poor and those in distress. In Deuteronomy 14:28–29, we are informed that one tenth of all products had to be given to the needy as a tithe every third year; while in Leviticus 19:9–10 and 23:22, it is related that one sixtieth of the gleanings and forgotten sheaves, as well as the topmost clusters of grapes, were left for those in need. Moreover, during such festivals as Passover, it was the custom

---

[1] Ephraim Frisch, *An Historical Survey of Jewish Philanthropy* (New York: McMillan, 1924), 10.

to invite the stranger, widow, and orphan to share food.[2] Again, in Exodus 22: 0–23 and 23:9 and also in Leviticus 19:23–34, it was mandatory that the stranger be respected and that the widow and orphan be treated with compassion.

Throughout the book of Psalms. there is expressed an overwhelming sympathy for the poor and those in want, while in the books of Proverbs, Job, and Ecclesiastes, charity and humanitarian acts are lauded: "Whoso mocketh the poor reproacheth his Maker,"[3] "God is the champion of the poor; their cry reaches him,"[4] and "He gives them their right."[5] "If you see in a province the poor oppressed and justice and right violently taken away, do not be amazed at the matter; for the high official is watched by a higher, and there are yet higher ones over them." [6] In Ecclesiastes one can also read, "Cast your bread upon the waters, for you will find it after many days. Give a portion to seven, or even to eight, for you know not what evil may happen on earth."[7]

Jewish biblical law made charity a personal obligation and brought a new standard to social life through the injunction found in Leviticus 19:18, "Thou shalt love thy neighbor as thyself." Charity was thus a religious duty incumbent upon all.

The Semitic historian Ephraim Frisch, in his monograph *An Historical Survey of Jewish Philanthropy,* observes that the ultimate obligation was to be obedient to the will of God.[8] Frisch reports that in the Mishnah, the ancient collection of utterances and enactments of the Israelites, deeds of loving kindness and other

---

[2] Deuteronomy 16:14

[3] Proverbs 17:5

[4] Job 34:28

[5] Job 36:6

[6] Ecclesiastes 5:8

[7] Ecclesiastes 11:1–2

[8] Frisch, *An Historical Survey of Jewish Philanthropy,* 85.

meritorious acts were to be rewarded not only in this world but also in the next; it was written that charity "averts the evil decree" or "saveth from death."[9]

Christianity, subsequently, came to view charity in this light: an outward manifestation of the reciprocal love between God and His creature. The depth of this love is expressed by St. Paul in one of the most eloquent and frequently quoted passages in the Bible:

> Though I speak with the tongues of men and of angels, and have not charity, I am become as sounding brass, or a tinkling cymbal.
>
> And though I have the gift of prophecy, and understand all mysteries, and all knowledge; and though I have all faith, so that I could remove mountains, and have not charity, I am nothing.
>
> And though I bestow all my goods to feed the poor, and though I give my body to be burned, and have not charity, it profiteth me nothing.
>
> Charity suffereth long, and is kind; charity envieth not; charity vaunteth not itself, is not puffed up,
>
> Doth not behave itself unseemly, seeketh not her own, is not easily provoked, thinketh no evil;
>
> Rejoiceth not in iniquity, but rejoiceth in the truth;
>
> Beareth all things, believeth all things, hopeth all things, endureth all things.
>
> Charity never faileth: but whether there be prophecies, they shall fail; whether there be

---

[9] Frisch, *An Historical Survey of Jewish Philanthropy*, 87.

tongues, they shall cease; whether there be knowledge, it shall vanish away.

For we know in part, and we prophesy in part.

But when that which is perfect is come, then that which is in part shall be done away.

When I was a child, I spake as a child, I understood as a child, I thought as a child: but when I became a man, I put away childish things.

For now we see through a glass, darkly; but then face to face: now I know in part; but then shall I know even as also I am known.

And now abideth faith, hope, charity, these three; but the greatest of these is charity.

—Corinthians 13:1

In its fundamental starkness, the biblical account of the sacrificial death of Christ in exchange for human immortality illustrates the ultimate expression of charity.

Charity testifies to our common humanity and reminds us of our shared fate. The biblical account of the Good Samaritan and the annunciation of the Seven Acts of Mercy—feeding the hungry, giving drink to the thirsty, providing shelter to the homeless, providing clothing for those without, visiting the prisoner, ransoming the captive, and burying the dead—stand as exemplary acts of charity.[10]

Notable examples of such conduct abound in Western society. History records the life of Saint Bridget of Ireland who displayed unusual courage and compassion in caring for the sick and the dying during the fifth century, a time marked by brutal

---

[10] Matthew 25:40ff.

atrocities, savage warfare, and pagan worship,[11] selfless actions that were later emulated by Brother Gerard of the Knights of St. John who risked his life in tending to the sick and wounded during the crusades.

The historian William McNeill observed in his book *Plagues and Peoples* that the teaching of the Christian gospel made life meaningful, even in the face of death. Not only could survivors find consolation in the vision of heavenly reunion with those who had died, but God's hand was also seen in the work of lifesaving caregivers. During the Black Plague of the fourteenth century, the caring for the sick and dying among Christians was a recognized religious duty. Elementary nursing care, even when all normal services had broken down, greatly reduced mortality. The simple provision of food and water allowed many persons to survive who would otherwise have perished.[12]

Brother Vincent de Paul and his Sisters of Charity in Paris are remembered for their boundless acts of charity, as is the humanitarian work of the Reverend Fleidner of Kaiserwerth Hospital in Prussia. Notable, too, is the life of the Belgian priest Father Damien, who died of leprosy contracted while caring for those afflicted with this disfiguring disease at the leper colony in Molokai, Hawaii. Mary Aikenhead is also recalled as the founder of the Irish Sisters of Charity in Dublin, the precursor to St. Christopher's Hospice of London, England, founded in the 1960s by Dame Cicely Saunders, the first of the modern-day hospices that are now located throughout the world. The list of charitable activities is endless.

---

[11] "St. Brigid of Ireland," Catholic Encyclopedia on-line, http://www.newadvent.org/cathen/02784b.htm (accessed February 2006).

[12] William McNeill, *Plagues and People* (Garden City, NY: Anchor Press, 1976), 108.

Wherever we may look, whatever mandate we might examine, the willingness to provide assistance or care to persons in need is as ancient as it is inspiring. In the Western world, such a calling can be traced to the idealism of the Old Testament Israelites and it is this tradition that the Puritans brought to the New World.

The historian Robert A. Gross observed in his article "Giving in America: From Charity to Philanthropy" that over the first 200 years of European settlement in North America the charitable ideal served as the embodiment of the godly community. Gross cites the sermon preached by John Winthrop prior to the Puritan's departure for Massachusetts Bay in 1630 in which Winthrop declared that the purpose of their journey was to establish a "City upon a Hill," a spiritual image taken from scripture that "conjured up not a physical place, but rather a spiritual ideal."[13] Inspired by divine grace and imbued with gospel love, the pilgrims saw themselves as brothers and sisters in Christ. Winthrop exhorted them to "delight in eache other and make others Condicions our owne, rejoyce together, mourne together, labour and suffer together, allwayes our Community as members of the same body."[14]

In this spirit, charity was not restricted to simply giving alms to the poor; it could take many forms: a simple gift, advice, or a kind word. In this light, everyone—rich and poor—could be, and was expected to be, charitable. Just as every individual was expected to behave altruistically, so every Puritan community was required to take care of its own inhabitants. As Gross explains:

---

[13] Robert A. Gross, "Giving in America: From Charity to Philanthropy," in *Charity, Philanthropy, and Civility in American History*, ed. Lawrence J. Friedman and Mark D. McGarvie (Cambridge: Cambridge University Press, 2003), 32.

[14] Gross, "Giving in America," 32.

There were no formal institutions—no poorhouses, hospitals, or asylums—in which to control and to segregate the dependent and the deviant. Normally, people were cared for in families, either their own or the households of others. As with foster care today, neighbors took in the aged, the sick, the orphaned, the indigent, and the helpless, and supplied their necessities at town expense. They also imposed discipline on the unruly: it was not uncommon for towns to subject village drunkards and even common criminals to the constraints of family. That was charity, too, provided for the individual's own good.[15]

While Puritan towns were prepared to assist their inhabitants who were in need, they were quick to discriminate between neighbor and stranger. The growth in population, the establishment of new settlements, and the increasing itinerancy of landless or jobless people not only put an unsupportable strain on the resources of a community but also came to challenge the effectiveness of individual charity itself.

In 1793, Philadelphia experienced an outbreak of yellow fever that overwhelmed the city's inhabitants.[16] The dying were abandoned; the dead went unburied; orphans and the elderly were left wandering the streets in search of food and shelter. According to the American historian J. H. Powell in his book *Bring Out Your Dead*, nearly all who could fled the city, including the president of the United States, leaving the victims of the fever to their fate. Among the few who remained, however, were Dr. Benjamin Rush (the father of American medicine and a

---

[15] Gross, "Giving in America," 33.
[16] J. H. Powell, *Bring Out Your Dead* (New York: Time, 1965).

cosigner of the Declaration of Independence), the mayor, a handful of medical colleagues and their assistants, and an appreciable number of clergy. They, together with a small and redoubtable number of ordinary laborers and craftsmen—including an umbrella maker—undertook the extraordinary task of maintaining law and order. In addition, they provided medical care, food, and shelter to the hungry and homeless, and gathered up and buried the dead. From reading Dr. Rush's diary and the voluminous correspondence covering the time of the epidemic, Powell concludes that what kept Dr. Rush and his band of dedicated volunteers at their posts, even though many of them were made ill by the fever and some died, was their sense of a benevolent duty inspired by the precepts of the Gospels.

It was in Philadelphia, according to Gross, that "the second tradition" of benevolence—philanthropy—emerged. Not only did civic-minded individuals, such as Benjamin Franklin, seek to meet the needs of those who were beyond the resources or reach of private individuals, but also through their efforts they promoted voluntary associations that attempted to advance the general well-being of the burgeoning nation. Benevolent associations such as the Quaker's Female Society for the Relief of the Distressed, the Evangelical Presbyterian's Female Association for the Relief of Women and Children, the Society for the Suppression of Vice, and the Female Orphan Asylum began to appear throughout America. In addition, there were formed marine societies, mechanic associations, Masonic lodges, charitable hospitals for the indigent, schools for the deaf, missionary societies, temperance associations, peace societies, and others.[17]

By 1820, Gross reports that upwards of 2,000 philanthropic organizations had been established throughout the country.

---

[17] Gross, "Giving in America," 40.

Their objectives were twofold: to serve God by good works and to serve society through practical public improvement.

Benjamin Franklin, for example, personally founded the first subscription library in the United States, a free school for poor children (that later became the University of Pennsylvania), the first volunteer fire company, and the first learned society: the American Philosophical Society. He firmly believed that "rational self-interest went hand in hand with the general good."[18] Traditional charity, on the other hand, was shortsighted and self-defeating. It was better, he thought, to inspire the poor with hope and provide them with the tools of self-support rather than offer them a charitable gift that would soon be dissipated. It was his conviction that organized philanthropic efforts could effectively ameliorate or even eliminate an oppressive condition.[19]

When Count Alexis de Tocqueville arrived in America in the 1830s, he was astounded at the number of voluntary associations that existed. De Tocqueville was initially sent to America by the French government to learn about the changes in the American penal system and the more humane practices concerning corporal punishment that had been mandated by the Eighth Amendment of the U.S. Constitution prohibiting "cruel and unusual punishment." He completed his investigation of American institutions, however, by singling out the volunteer association as the quintessential American institution. In his historical report *Democracy in America,* de Tocqueville saw these organizations as energizing the young democracy while providing a culture that both promoted and supported constructive public enterprises. This was not so, he observed, in

---

[18] Gross, "Giving in America," 38.

[19] Benjamin Franklin, *The Autobiography of Benjamin Franklin* (New York: McMillan, 1927), 172.

the Old World where noblesse oblige was the norm and benevolence, in the tradition of Good King Wenceslas, was largely in the hands of an indolent and, more often, indifferent aristocracy.[20]

What was called an "Age of Benevolence" (1790–1840) gave the work of charity both a new structure and focus. Philanthropy, henceforth, was to be exercised mainly through formal volunteer associations rather than left in the hands of fickle donors; it was to address more "rationally" the social, educational, religious, and cultural needs of the whole community, rather than a particular problem confronting a single individual. The goal of philanthropy became, ultimately, to eliminate the conditions or circumstances that gave rise to the problems rather than simply addressing the symptoms.

New developments in American society soon changed this promising formula. According to Gross, the upswell of religious zeal associated with what was termed the "Second Great Awakening," redirected charity toward bestowing the "spiritual food" of Christ and away from the soup kitchen and the provision of other basic needs. It was the soul and not the body that was the "one thing needful."[21] Moreover, the disruptive forces of emerging industrial capitalism served to diminish the zeal for charity as the social classes became physically and more sociologically distant from one another. The dependent, the derelict, and the deviant came to be seen as more personally responsible for their circumstances, given the bountiful opportunities that the burgeoning economy offered, while the bureaucratic nature of volunteer organizations weakened the relationship between donor and recipient. Sympathy for the

---

[20] Alexis de Tocqueville, *Democracy in America* (Garden City, NY: Doubleday, 1969), 514.

[21] Gross, "Giving in America," 42.

poor and destitute waned. At the same time, it came to be seen as humanitarian to separate marginalized or stigmatized people from the greater society and confine them to prison, hospital, or asylum as conducive to their personal well-being and moral enlightenment.[22]

Illustrative of this shift from the idea of personal charity to impersonal philanthropy is the distinctively different efforts of two prominent leaders in the field, Jane Addams and John D. Rockefeller Sr. A leading Christian reformer, Addams was dismayed by the grim living conditions associated with the new industrial age and, in response, established a settlement house—the now famous Hull House—in Chicago. Her intention was twofold: to provide useful services to the new immigrant as well as to others in need and to acquaint privileged young men and women to the harsh realities of modern life while providing them with a practical and beneficial outlet for their compassionate sentiments.

As the founder of Standard Oil, Rockefeller, on the other hand, by virtue of the magnitude of his wealth and the number of supplicants, was obliged to turn his gift-giving over to professional consultants and managers. This insulating layer between giver and gift not only gave impetus to the practice of what came to be called "scientific" gift-giving but gave rise also to two new professions: the philanthropic foundation executive and the modern-day social worker.[23] These developments also stimulated the proliferation of nonprofit institutions that are now an integral part of American society.

---

[22] Gross, "Giving in America," 43.

[23] Roy E. Finkenbine, "Law, Reconstruction, and African American Education in the Post-Emancipation South," in *Charity, Philanthropy, and Civility in American History*, ed. Lawrence J. Friedman and Mark D. McGarvie (Cambridge: Cambridge University Press, 2003), 172.

These changes, however, did not mean the end of personal charity. Individual acts of benevolence have never been eliminated by corporate or impersonal philanthropy. Olivia Sage, for instance, a deeply religious woman and the widow of the Wall Street financier Russell Sage, following his death in 1906 established the Russell Sage Foundation with an initial donation of $10 million. She continued to be involved—personally—throughout her long life in private acts of charity. Her immediate benevolence represented the ideal of biblical stewardship, even as it stood at the crossroads of traditional private gift-giving and the new scientific beneficence represented by the emerging philanthropic foundations.[24]

Before the establishment of the Russell Sage Foundation, there were approximately two dozen charitable foundations in the United States. While some foundations sought "the improvement of living conditions in the United States" and centered their attention in several areas including child welfare, city planning, and industrial relations, others were single-purpose foundations. The Rosenwald Fund, for instance, centered its efforts solely on the improvement of race relations in the United States, as did the earlier Peabody Education Fund, established in 1867 to aid the postwar South. The John F. Slater Fund for the Education of Freedmen was dedicated to the education of former slaves.[25] The Milbank and Commonwealth

---

[24] Ruth Crocker, "From Gift to Foundation: The Philanthropic Lives of Mrs. Russell Sage," in *Charity, Philanthropy, and Civility in American History*, ed. Lawrence J. Friedman and Mark D. McGarvie (Cambridge: Cambridge University Press, 2003), 200.

[25] Finkenbine, "Law, Reconstruction, and African American Education," 168.

Funds, on the other hand, worked to promote new ideas and practices in the area of public health.[26]

The charter that allows philanthropic foundations to exist and function separate from government is rooted in the Contract Clause of the U.S. Constitution (Article I, Section 10), which states, "No law should be passed impairing the obligation owing to contract." This clause ensures that private contract rights take precedence over public interests.[27] Churches and religious institutions (as incorporated entities) as well as the foundations established by individuals, families, and business corporations are seen, therefore, as legally separate from the public domain and not subject to state governance. This opinion was upheld in 1819 in the landmark case of the *Trustees of Dartmouth College v. Woodward,* in which the Supreme Court ruled that the incorporation of Dartmouth College (a religiously endowed institution at the time) was, in effect, a new entity and as such possessed attributes similar to that of an individual. To wit: persons representing an incorporated enterprise were to be considered as a single individual possessing the right of contract in perpetuity.[28] The implications of this decision resonate to the present, and corporations and individuals, or their families, are essentially free from oversight and state government control to pursue their own business as well as charitable programs.

In 1913 Congress ratified the Sixteenth Amendment, allowing the federal government to tax both the income of individuals as well as the profits of corporations. It was only in

---

[26] Finkenbine, "Law, Reconstruction, and African American Education," 225.

[27] Mark D. McGarvie, "The Dartmouth College Case and the Legal Design of Civil Society," in *Charity, Philanthropy, and Civility in American History,* ed. Lawrence J. Friedman and Mark D. McGarvie (Cambridge: Cambridge University Press, 2003), 99.

[28] McGarvie, "The Dartmouth College Case," 101.

1935 following the revision of the Federal Tax Act that wealthy individuals such as Carnegie and Rockefeller had strong monetary incentives to establish a tax-exempt foundation.[29]

The federal government's tax policies resulted in a surge in the establishment of new foundations. Randall Holcombe, in his account of this development, reports that during the 1980s over 3,000 foundations were established, each with assets in excess of $1 million, while the 1990s saw the creation of thousands more.[30]

In 2006, according to the annual report on philanthropy *Giving USA,* approximately $295 billion was given to various groups, organizations, and institutions. Private philanthropic foundations, together with corporate foundations, made grants totaling somewhat more than $36 billion, approximately 12 percent of the total amount. Living individuals contributed more than $222 billion, or 75 percent of the total amount. Bequests totaled $22 billion, or 7 percent, while grants from corporations were estimated at 12 billion dollars, or 4 percent of the total.[31]

Religious organizations were the largest group of beneficiaries, receiving approximately 32 percent of the grants. Education received 13 percent, while grants to foundations and health received approximately 6 percent and 10 percent, respectively, of the overall allocations. Grants made to the arts, culture, and humanities totaled approximately 4 percent, as did public-society benefit grants, which includes support for civil rights programs and community development. Environmental

---

[29] Judith Sealander, "Curing Evils at Their Source: The Arrival of Scientific Giving," in *Charity, Philanthropy, and Civility in American History,* ed. Lawrence J. Friedman and Mark D. McGarvie (Cambridge: Cambridge University Press, 2003), 226.

[30] Sealander, "Curing Evils at Their Source," 226.

[31] *Giving USA Foundation 2007* (Indianapolis, IN: Center on Philanthropy at Indiana University), 15

programs and international affairs programs accounted for approximately 2 percent and 3 percent, respectively, of the gift giving, while unallocated giving amounted to $26 billion or about 8 percent of the total.[32]

The total assets of the twenty leading private foundations in the United States amounted to somewhat more than $159 billion in 2006.

As H. Peter Karoff, founder of the Philanthropic Initiative and presently the senior fellow at Tufts University College of Citizenship and Public Service, reported in his recent book *Just Money: A Critique of Contemporary American Philanthropy*, private foundations "represent the largest pool of private capital available in the world that is free from both the constraints of government and the marketplace."[33]

Philanthropy is big business. According to Professor Karoff, in 2002 there were more than 60,000 private philanthropic foundations operating in the United States. The so-called independent sector, which represents more than a million nonprofit organizations of all descriptions, reported in 2003 an expenditure, in the aggregate, of almost a quarter of a trillion dollars.[34] Some critics are concerned about this growth and believe that as a consequence so-called scientific philanthropy threatens to become separated from traditional charity both in terms of personal contact and purpose. Professor Karoff's own point of view, moreover, would appear to embody this shift. He insinuates in his account of the history of charity that modern philanthropy is the result of personal decisions on the part of wealthy donors rather than acknowledging its longstanding

---

[32] *Giving USA Foundation 2007*, 16

[33] Peter H. Karoff, *Just Money: A Critique of Contemporary American Philanthropy* (Boston: Philanthropic Initiative, 2004), xv.

[34] Karoff, *Just Money*, xvi.

religious history and ethical roots.[35] The economist Randall Holcombe, too, in his discussion of the origins and development of foundations, *Writing off Ideas*, would have us believe that philanthropy finds its origins in Greece rather than with the Old Testament Israelites, by crediting Plato as the original source of the charitable tradition. Reportedly Plato bequeathed his estate to his own academy in 300 BCE.[36]

To my mind, these modern-day spokespeople for scientific philanthropy, by mischaracterizing the history of charitable giving in Western society, minimize its moral and ethical basis and, ironically, potentially weaken the very social bonds that philanthropy purports to strengthen. By denying or diminishing the historic ethical and religious traditions, there is serious risk that the charitably minded donor will turn his back on what has always been considered a moral obligation and instead embrace an attitude of noblesse oblige, as de Tocqueville recounted in the case of France, where charity was essentially equated with caprice.

There is no question that the private foundations of America have greatly contributed to the welfare of the country. One can readily recall the extraordinary generosity and personal involvement of Olivia Sage or the munificence of Andrew Carnegie, who in addition to other gifts, established more than 2,800 public libraries in cities and towns throughout America. The Rockefeller Foundation is remembered for its establishment of the University of Chicago, the reconstruction of the historic town of Williamsburg, and the monumental role it played in the establishment of the national parks system. Such gifts have enhanced the nation, even as they have improved the cultural

---

[35] Karoff, *Just Money*, xvi.

[36] Randall G. Holcombe, *Writing Off Ideas* (New Brunswick, NJ: Transaction, 2000), 25

and intellectual life of its citizenry. It is also important to point out that these extraordinary gestures were made before the implementation of the federal income tax system that now allows for a tax deduction in return for such open-handed generosity.[37]

Philanthropic foundations, as nonprofit organizations, must meet certain conditions of the tax code. Essentially, they are required to undertake a certain level of expenditure (on average, 5 percent of assets), comply with certain forms of disclosure, and avoid certain types of activities—in exchange for which a donor can bequeath his estate to his family foundation and be exempt from death duties and other related taxes.[38]

Critics express concern regarding the governance, accountability, and transparency of private family foundations. Moreover, as some foundations have moved into the realm of making or influencing public policy—both domestic and foreign—questions have been raised regarding what the proper role of private foundations should be in a democratic society.

Some argue that private philanthropy should do only what the government cannot do when resources are limited. Others question the role of private philanthropy in promoting new or experimental social engineering programs altogether and instead would restrict philanthropy to addressing the more customary needs of the sick and poor. Karoff explains that philanthropic organizations are caught today in the middle of contentious political and ideological debates, even as they wrestle with charges of violating the public trust or confront the threat of reform legislation that has been proposed in response to recent scandals.[39] He claims that since the Reagan administration,

---

[37] Sealander, "Curing Evils at Their Source."

[38] Holcombe, *Writing Off Ideas*, 20

[39] Karoff, *Just Money*, xviii.

private foundations have been encouraged—indeed, been given incentives—to do more on behalf of society, as the role of government has devolved from federal to state and local authority.[40] To be sure, as he says, "the field of philanthropy is undergoing immense change."[41] Not only has the number of new foundations increased enormously in the past few decades, but they also wish to exercise their individual interests in a manner oftentimes different from past practice.[42] Indeed, some affluent individuals choose not to endow a foundation at all but simply make gifts and grants, which invites the question as to the rationale of allowing private tax-exempt foundations to exist at all.

Critics are particularly concerned that the private foundation support of so-called think tanks—such as the CATO Institute, the Heritage Foundation, the Hoover Institute, or the American Enterprise Institute—can have an undue influence on the American political process. The lack of oversight and the absence of accountability allows for the promotion and support of interests that have been shown to be antidemocratic. For example, Russ Bellant, in his book *The Coors Connection: How Coors Family Philanthropy Undermines Democratic Pluralism*, charges that "the Coors family philanthropy aims a financial silver bullet at the heart of democratic pluralism in the United States."[43]

The Coors family has long been a major donor to different social, political, and educational projects that have reflected their strongly held conservative views. According to Bellant, the Coors family has funded organizations that believe in Christian segregated schools and has supported groups associated with

---

[40] Karoff, *Just Money*, xvii.

[41] Karoff, *Just Money*, xviii.

[42] Karoff, *Just Money*, xviii.

[43] Russ Bellant, *The Coors Connection: How Coors Family Philanthropy Undermines Democratic Pluralism* (Boston: South End Press, 1991), v.

the Reverend Sun Myung Moon, who has called for "the abolition of American democracy and the establishment of a theocratic state."[44]

The Coors family, Bellant reports, has long been active in promoting public policy initiatives. In 1980, through the Heritage Foundation, it published *Mandate for Leadership*, which was intended to provide political advice to the new Reagan administration. Among its many recommendations was increased support for the military and intelligence agencies, and reduced spending for education, welfare, and health. This is but one example of how private foundations, without oversight or accountability, can challenge the stability and well-being of the polity.[45]

After reviewing the Coors Family Foundation's social policies and political activities, both domestic and foreign, Bellant concludes:

> [The] family aids and abets a network of conservative and far right groups including those which seek to turn back civil rights, destroy trade unions, disregard the fragility of the environment, and promote racial bigotry, homophobia and male supremacy....
>
> In pursuit of its political agenda, the Coors family network employs or is allied with secretive, authoritarian, and totalitarian political and religious forces which overlap with racist and anti-Semitic elements, all pushing programs which would result in the diminution or

---

44 Bellant, *The Coors Connection*, xv.
45 Bellant, *The Coors Connection*, 9.

dissolution of pluralism and democracy in the United States.[46]

Teresa Odendahl, moreover, observes in her book *Charity Begins at Home: Generosity and Self-Interest among the Philanthropic Elite,* that "elite American philanthropy serves the interests of the rich to a greater extent than it does the interests of the poor, disadvantaged, or disabled."[47] She makes this observation in the light of her personal interviews with 140 millionaire philanthropists and the modest amount (approximately 5 percent per year) reportedly distributed through their foundations in relation to their overall assets. Moreover, many of the philanthropists, she reports, demonstrate a narrow focus in their giving. The Getty Foundation, for example, makes grants only to the Getty Museum. Their patronage, therefore, is primarily directed toward the cultural interests of a select clientele, to the virtual exclusion of all others.

An article in the *New York Times* recently shed further light on the ethically questionable or illegal practices surrounding such philanthropic activity. It reports that a donor established a philanthropic entity called a "supporting organization" with a donation of $1 billion. This permitted him to avoid taxes on much of his income for a period of time. However, at the time of the report, little of the money ($3.4 million) went to charity, the remainder being held by the entity. Supporting organizations, the article explains, are attractive to benefactors because they offer generous tax benefits without entailing burdensome requirements. By agreeing to relinquish control over his money, a donor, since he can appoint the organization's

---

[46] Bellant, *The Coors Connection*, 103.

[47] Teresa Odendahl, *Charity Begins at Home: Generosity and Self-Interest among the Philanthropic Elite* (New York: Basic Books, 1990), 3.

board, can retain appreciable control over it. Critics complain that many wealthy people today make use of such tax arrangements to shelter their wealth, rather than any charitable use.[48]

Such a pattern of behavior leaves open the question as to whether or not the country would be better off if the government were to return to a different tax formula, which today, in its current form, weighs heavily in favor of the wealthy.

Waldemar Nielsen, a recognized expert on the workings of philanthropic foundations, observed in his book *The Golden Donors* that:

> ...in the great jungle of American democracy and capitalism there is no more strange or improbable creature than the private foundation. Private foundations are virtually a denial of basic premise: aristocratic institutions living on the privileges and indulgence of an egalitarian society; aggregations of private wealth, which, contrary to the proclaimed instincts of Economic Man, have been conveyed to public purposes. Like the giraffe, they could not possibly exist, but they do.

The question facing the United States today is the extraordinary shift that has occurred in the contemporary functioning of private foundations with respect to their stated purposes and goals and the role they play in our pluralistic, democratic society. There is no question that American society has greatly benefited in the past from the private foundation, as well as from the less publicized efforts of nonprofit charitable organizations. But now, more than ever, it needs the selfless

---

[48] Stephanie Strom, "A Tax Benefit That Bypasses Idea of Charity," *New York Times*, April 5, 2005, 1.

participation of what is presently called the independent sector, a participation that in addition to being relevant and compassionate must also be accountable and transparent if it is to continue to enjoy the public's trust.[49]

As Frisch reminds us, it was Jewish biblical law that made charity a human obligation for which all were accountable, for it was recognized even in that early time that "the basic cause of poverty, misery and injustice in the world was due to human greed."[50]

Originally, the practice of charity within the Judeo-Christian worldview had as its primary motivation the shared love of God and the joy that comes from being an agent of His beneficence. Implicit in this paradigm was the promise of immortality. Today, scientific philanthropy is not only in danger of losing this historic religious vision but is driven by the burdensome tax codes and laws of inheritance. The issue, however, is not simply either/or. The issue, rather, is whether allowing the private family foundations to operate as they do is the most cost-effective and efficient way to address the compelling social issues that presently confront American society. The question is: Can the country afford to be denied the billions of taxable dollars that presently find their way into sheltered family trusts that could otherwise be used to advance the well-being of the commonweal? As we have noted, the overwhelming percentage of charitable gift-giving by private foundations is to middle- and upper-class institutions. Less than 6 percent of the more than $240 billion dollars was contributed to programs or organizations that addressed the problems of health,

---

[49] Jerome L. Himmelstein, *Looking Good and Doing Good: Corporate Philanthropy and Corporate Power* (Bloomington: University of Indiana Press, 1997), 31

[50] Frisch, *An Historical Survey of Jewish Philanthropy*, 23.

employment, education, or housing. In the case of the Getty Foundation, for instance, with an endowment of over $9 billion, the entirety of their gift giving is made to support the Getty Museum. But such egregious, singularly self-serving acts of philanthropy pale in comparison to the much more compelling political issues.

The Coors Foundation's activities, as related by Bellant, are a case in point. In stark contrast, the munificence of a Bill Gates or a Warren Buffet in their efforts to stem the AIDS pandemic testifies to the fact that the independent sector, potentially, has the will and determination to act benignly on behalf of the nation. Exceptions to their example constitute a challenging problem for our democratic institutions. The question is: how long can the American body politic afford to tolerate the unaccounted and unsupervised possession of great wealth in the hands of those whose social philosophy and political action threaten to undermine the principles and institutions upon which our democratic society rests?

Charity was inspired, as Frisch reports, by God's love for humankind and by the divine directive to "love thy neighbor as thyself," a command made further compelling by the prospect of personal immortality if one is compliant. There are those, however, who argue that philanthropy derives less from this theological vision and more from Plato's generous example of endowing his own academy. Still others claim it expresses the principle of *noblesse oblige*—the rich have an obligation to the poor—that is embodied in the traditional Christmas carol *Good King Wenceslas*. With the introduction of a national income tax in 1913, a significant change took place that gave rise to what is termed "scientific philanthropy" that essentially transformed the manner as well as the purpose and intention of giving. Around the time of the Second World War, with the increasing tax rates that the war engendered, the motivation for charitable giving gave rise to a second goal: the avoidance of substantial death and estate duties.

I would suggest that the consequences of this change can be seen in the law that permits the taxpayer who has established his or her personal foundation to withhold ninety-five cents out of every taxable dollar on condition that he or she distributes the remaining five cents to a recognizable charity. To my mind, two things are lost here: first, the retained taxable monies that could otherwise go into the nation's coffers, and second, the communal sense represented by the sharing of one's wealth with the poor and needy. Since the time of President Reagan, especially, the government has actively promoted the idea that charitable activities should increasingly be the responsibility of state and local governments in loose collaboration with the private sector. At the same time, the extraordinary expansion of wealth in the hands of private individuals has given rise to an unprecedented increase in the number of family foundations. The question is, is this charity or is it a form of fraud? Under the guise of "doing good," citizens who can afford to establish a family foundation can also expect, under this system of taxation, to do very well—but at whose expense?

There are many who take strong exception to this point of view. They are not sanguine that the government is in a better position to address need in the United States than are the private foundations. They ask the relevant question: Would the additional monies made available to the nation's treasury if the tax laws were revised necessarily find their way to those in need? The failure of the government's response to the Katrina disaster is a telling case in point. The agencies of the government were unprepared for the magnitude of the disaster and egregiously inept and incompetent in their response to it. The local nature of many family foundations, permits them flexibility and, frequently, a better understanding of how to address a particular social concern. In any event, the question of the role of the private family foundation and the costs and benefits associated with its multiple involvements and activities needs to be aggressively addressed.

Chapter 7:
War

Onward Christian Soldiers

Onward Christian soldiers, marching as to war,
With the cross of Jesus going on before.
At the sign of triumph Satan's host doth flee;
On then, Christian soldiers, on to victory!
…
Hell's foundations quiver at the shout of praise;
Brothers lift your voices, loud your anthems raise.
…
Crowns and thrones may perish, kingdoms rise and wane,
But the church of Jesus constant will remain.
Gates of hell can never gainst that church prevail;
We have Christ's own promise, and that cannot fail.

—Words by Sabine Baring-Gould (1865)
Music by Sir Arthur S. Sullivan (1871)

War within the Judeo-Christian tradition has always been portrayed as an instrument of faith. Since Abraham confronted his enemy King Chedor-Laomar and was assured by God "to have no fear [for] I am your shield," to the prophesized second battle of the end, as described in the Book of Revelations, where God will finally defeat Satan and his minions, Christian theology has characterized war as a confrontation between good and evil.[1] For a Christian, therefore, to give up his life in defense of his faith is to die in defiance of death; he believes that spiritual reunion with God—immortality—awaits his willing sacrifice.

War has taken a variety of forms. There have been wars of conquest that were the result of intense population growth. History records the incursions of the Macedonians, under the leadership of Alexander the Great, who conquered much of the land between Egypt and India in the fourth century BCE; it recounts the Germanic tribes led by Attila the Hun, who later in the fifth century CE vandalized the Roman Empire.[2] History records the exploits of the marauding Vikings, and the recurrent invasions of the Celts who terrorized European cities throughout the eighth to eleventh centuries with the skulls of their defeated enemies rattling from their horses' saddles.[3] The twelfth and thirteenth centuries saw the Mongols, under the Khans, occupy the fertile lands of eastern Europe, ruthlessly pillaging and ravishing indigenous populations as they proceeded.

History has been witness to human conflict in the form of wars of liberation, such as the American Revolution, and wars of ideology, in which nations with competing political philosophies engaged in hostilities. The Second World War with the unremitting bombing of such European cities as London,

---

[1] Genesis 14:17; Revelations 21:7–10.

[2] Jerry Clemens King, "The Role of War in History," *War and the Human Race*, ed. Maurice N. Walsh (Amsterdam: Elsevier, 1971), 63.

[3] La Barre, *Muelos*, 16.

Coventry, Dresden, and Berlin, and the obliteration of the Japanese cities of Hiroshima and Nagasaki by atomic bombs, characterize such wars.

There have been economic wars. The invasion of Manchuria by the Japanese in the 1930s was reputedly to obtain the natural resources that Japan sought for its burgeoning industrial economy.[4]

Over the centuries, history has witnessed religious wars such as the Muslim conquests of the lands extending from Iran to France in the eighth century and the Crusades, wars waged against Islam by Christian Europe during the eleventh to the thirteenth centuries;[5] while the seventeenth century experienced the Thirty Years' War between European Protestants and Catholics. This past century records the calamitous religious conflict between Muslim and Hindu following India's independence in 1947, in which millions of men, women, and children were uprooted from their homes in the midst of violence and bloodshed.[6]

Today we are reluctant witnesses to a series of localized wars in Afghanistan, Algeria, Burundi, Colombia, the Congo, Indonesia, India, Iraq, Liberia, Nigeria, Pakistan, Peru, the Philippines, Russia, Somalia, Sudan and Uganda, and witness to wanton terrorist acts that continue to inflame the world.[7]

In categorizing these different forms of communal conflict, I wish to make the point that the nationally organized episodes of mass killing recorded throughout history are not necessarily the same, either as to cause, intent, or form. The one reality that is

---

[4] *New Encyclopaedia Britannica, Macropeaedia,* vol. 2, 437.

[5] King, "The Role of War in History," 63–64.

[6] Stoessinger, *Why Nations Go to War,* 117.

[7] Chris Hedges, *What Every Person Should Know about War* (New York: Free Press, 2003), 2.

constant is the propensity for human beings to engage in periodic homicidal behavior.

History bears witness to such a conclusion. According to Chris Hedges, in his book *What Every Person Should Know about War,* over the past 3,400 years of recorded history, humans have been entirely at peace for only 268 years or 8 percent of the time.[8] Moreover, the American psychiatrist Maurice N. Walsh has calculated the intervals of peace for a select group of nations: Russia, United States, England, France and Germany. He found that they have engaged in war on average every 19.65 years or approximately once every generation since the last quarter of the eighteenth century. Specifically, the intervals of peace for the different nations were: Russia 17.74; United States, 18.00; England, 18.42; France, 19.85; and Germany, 23.8.[9] How does one account for this disturbing record? Why do we go to war virtually every generation despite our avowed preference to live in peace and in the face of the divine directive "Thou shalt not kill"?

In the early centuries of Judeo-Christian thought, war was believed to be the scourge of a wrathful God, like pestilence, famine, and plague.[10] St. Augustine (354–430 CE) considered the human propensity for war as a result of God's will to rebuke humankind and to remind them of their weakness and utter dependence on Him.[11] By the sixteenth century, the English philosopher Thomas Hobbes embraced a more secular perspective. He found the reason for war in the unbridled

---

[8] Hedges, *What Every Person Should Know about War*, 1.

[9] Maurice N. Walsh, "Psychic Factors in the Causation of Recurrent Mass Homicide," in *War and the Human Race*, ed. Maurice N. Walsh (Amsterdam: Elsevier, 1971), 78.

[10] King, "The Role of War in History," 62.

[11] Keith L. Nelson and Spencer C. Olin Jr. *Why War? Ideology, Theory, and History* (Berkeley: University of California Press, 1979), 18.

hubris, ambition, and other passions that make up human nature.[12]

Although Charles Darwin in his paradigm-shattering book *Origin of the Species* did not explicitly address human aggression or humankind's penchant for war, two schools of thought emerged from his writings that drew contrary conclusions regarding his revolutionary biological theories. On the one hand, Darwin's concept of natural selection became a cause for optimism for those who believed that the human race was destined to lift itself morally above the practice of war; while on the other hand, his concept of the survival of the fittest led others to believe that humankind was destined forever to be burdened by perpetual conflict.[13]

In the aftermath of Darwin's theory of evolution, it was believed that human aggression, like anatomical structure, was something that humankind inherited along with the rest of the animal world.[14] Following the pioneering efforts of leading observers of animal behavior such as Konrad Lorenz, it became clear that aggression, like any other behavioral trait, is species specific. Ethnologists do not believe, for instance, that it constitutes aggressive behavior when a lion attacks its prey. Animals have no feelings one way or another about their prey; they kill simply to survive. Moreover, aggressive behavior in animals, ethnologists have determined, is situation specific. Aggression in birds, for example, is limited to three particular issues: protection of individual breeding territory, selection of

---

[12] Thomas Hobbes, Leviathan (Oxford: Clarendon Press, 1909), chap. 14.

[13] Nelson and Olin, *Why War?*, 20.

[14] Nelson and Olin, *Why War?*, 26.

optimal mates, and defense of the young.[15] This is found to be true in general for solitary, nongregarious animals. Human beings, on the other hand, are social, nonsolitary creatures and—while they, too, possess innate aggressive tendencies and to that extent are one with other animals—they have also experienced a cultural evolution that in many respects overrides their biological inheritance. Ethnologists believe, therefore, that humans have an opportunity denied other animals—namely, they can monitor their behavior by their ability to assess the outcome of their actions. Simply stated: human aggression, while basically rooted in biology, need not necessarily bind humankind to a state of perpetual conflict. At a special plenary session of the American Anthropological Association in 1967, it was resolved that the cause of war could not be found in animal ethnology. As the English anthropologist Ashley Montagu observed: "The development of intelligence increasingly freed man from the bondage of biologically predetermined response mechanisms.... Far from being innate, human aggressiveness is a learned form of behavior."[16]

Other theories of war abound. In the more recent era, Freud proposed a psychological theory of war in his famous correspondence with Albert Einstein, *Why War?,* in which he attributed human aggression to the lust of destruction, which he termed the death-instinct, and like the concept of original sin, accompanied one's birth.[17] Freud was later obliged to modify this view, bowing to his critics who challenged this reductionist

---

[15] Herbert Friedmann, "Animal Aggression and Its Implications for Human Behavior," in *War and the Human Race,* ed. Maurice N. Walsh (Amsterdam: Elsevier, 1971), 25–29.

[16] Lawrence LeShan, *The Psychology of War: Comprehending Its Mystique and Its Madness* (New York: Helios Press, 2002), 15.

[17] Sigmund Freud, "Why War?" in *The Complete Psychological Works of Sigmund Freud,* vol. 22 (London: Hogarth Press, 1964), 45.

theory. It was argued that war is not known in all human societies, and that some societies—Sweden, for example, renowned for its warlike character—has failed to support Freud's hypothetical death-instinct by not going to war for the past 150 years.

Karl Marx believed that the capitalist system itself, with its invidious and divisive class system, is fundamentally responsible for war. He believed that the human propensity for war will not end until nations are prepared to relinquish the idea of private property, which places individual rights above those of society.[18]

Other theorists lay the cause of war at the feet of the manufacturers of the weapons of war, the so-called merchants of death. Some argue that these industrialists promote wars in order to sell their lethal wares. Others have proposed that speculators in the search for profits provoke political incidents that incite war between nations. It has been suggested that it was the private investments of Russian entrepreneurs in the Yalu River area that ignited the Russo-Japanese War of 1904–1905, much to the subsequent detriment to the Russian state.[19]

Joseph Schumpeter, an Austrian economist, contended that war between nations is mainly fostered by a nation's ruling class in order to maintain its authority and dominance, as well as by those who stand to gain financially or socially from a war policy.[20] Clausewitz, on the other hand, in his classic treatise *On War*, viewed war as simply an extension of diplomacy calculated to seek the most favorable economic circumstances for a people.[21]

---

[18] Nelson and Olin, *Why War?*, 71.

[19] Bernard Brodie, "Theories on the Causes of War," in *War and the Human Race*, ed. Maurice N. Walsh (Amsterdam: Elsevier, 1971), 14.

[20] Nelson and Olin, *Why War?*, 60.

[21] Karl von Clausewitz, *On War* (New York: Everyman's Library, 1993).

More recently, the American economist Seymour Melman, in his book *Pentagon Capitalism,* argued that the cause of war—specifically the Vietnam War—could be traced not to the actions of entrepreneurial capitalists or an entrenched plutocracy, but rather to the ascendancy of the United States military in the form of a military-industrial complex of which President Eisenhower warned the nation in his farewell address.[22] For Melman, the Vietnam War was an outgrowth of just such an emergence—a military state within a state that has given birth to an "institutionalized power lust."[23]

There are also theories as to the cause of war within the field of social science. One social-psychological theory identifies certain war-minded individuals as pathological and fanatical in their perceived missions. According to Walsh, dictators such as Hitler, Stalin, and Mussolini demonstrated comparable behavior characteristics and presented personality profiles that have been perceived to be lacking in normal guilt feelings or normal emotions of love and tenderness.[24]

The structural-functional theory of war differs more in emphasis than in kind from the social-psychological perspective. It attempts to explain war and other dislocating conflicts without reference to the individual or to psychological factors per se. The structural-functional theory conceives the social system as being constituted of interdependent structures that accommodate each other. Echoing the theories of war put forward by the classical liberals of the eighteenth and nineteenth centuries (John Stewart Mill and others), this theory assumes that society is essentially self-regulating and that there would be

---

[22] *Eisenhower's Farewell Address to the Nation,* January 17, 1961.

[23] Nelson and Olin, *Why War?,* 62.

[24] Walsh, "Psychic Factors in the Causation of Recurrent Mass Homicide," 79.

little cause for war if the economic system was left to itself without government interference. As economic cooperation would be to the benefit of all, it would serve as a rational substitute for war. Human conflict is thus explained by structural-functionalists as a transitory malfunction of the domestic system such as the installation of a military-minded government or the absence of a stable, integrated international system.[25]

Group conflict theory holds, on the other hand, that war is the result of society and/or the international order being inherently competitive for the world's limited resources. As a consequence, coercive relationships inevitably will prevail among peoples and nations. The avoidance of war, according to this theory, is essentially a function of ensuring that a balance of power will be maintained through such organizations as the League of Nations or, currently, the United Nations.[26]

Importantly, an idea that has resonated down through the ages contends that war is fundamentally beneficial for humankind. The classical Roman poet Juvenal, for instance, is quoted as saying: "Now we suffer the evils of long peace. Luxury hatches terrors worse than wars,"[27] while the eighteenth-century German philosopher Hegel opined, "War has the higher meaning that through it…the ethical health of nations is maintained."[28] One of the leading German generals of the First World War, Helmuth Johannes Ludwig von Moltke, furthermore placed war within the mythic tradition. He declared, "War is an integral part of God's ordering of the universe. In War, man's noblest virtues come into play: courage and

---

[25] Nelson and Olin, *Why War?*, 51–57.
[26] Nelson and Olin, *Why War?*, 58–60.
[27] LeShan, *The Psychology of War*, 16.
[28] LeShan, *The Psychology of War*, 16.

renunciation, fidelity to duty and a readiness for sacrifice that does not stop short of offering up life itself. Without war, the world would become swamped in materialism."[29]

John J. Pershing, von Moltke's counterpart as commanding general of the U.S. Army, was much more succinct when he was asked why men go to war; he is said to have replied, "Because they enjoy it."[30]

As the distinguished American psychologist Lawrence LeShan sardonically observed, "There is definitely something about war that appeals to human beings."[31] In his book *The Psychology of War: Comprehending Its Mystique and Its Madness*, LeShan explored what that something is. It is his conclusion that, depending upon the circumstances, human beings are predisposed to use one of two alternate perceptions of reality that he describes as sensory (rational) or mythic (irrational). Sensory reality he defines as the common-sense perception that embraces the experiential world of everyday life. As he says, "It is the form of reality we in the West ordinarily think of as the real one. It is the reality in which we tie our shoelaces…in which we purchase airplane tickets and take taxis."[32] It is, he explains further, simply a practical problem to be attended to within the context of temporal causal relationships.

Mythic reality, on the other hand, is the belief in the intervention of higher powers and the efficacy of prayer or magic in influencing human affairs. In the face of a medical crisis, a person with a sensory perception of reality would, in all likelihood, call a physician or go to the emergency room of a hospital for treatment; a person who entertains a mythic

---

[29] LeShan, *The Psychology of War*, 16.

[30] LeShan, *The Psychology of War*, 117.

[31] LeShan, *The Psychology of War*, 72.

[32] LeShan, *The Psychology of War*, 43.

perception of reality might, in addition to using such practical medical services, also resort to prayer, superstitious formulas, or magic, in much the same way that one would cross his or her fingers for good luck.[33]

In his analysis of the way in which human beings think that can lead to war, LeShan attempted a comparison of the way reality is viewed in peacetime as compared to wartime. He found the differences in perception to be striking. His observations (paraphrased) are as follows:

1. In peacetime, groups with different ideas are generally tolerated; in wartime, critical issues are simply polarized into right or wrong, and no middle ground is tolerated.

2. In peacetime, the present is viewed as fairly much like the past, with differences essentially quantitative. In wartime, the situation is qualitatively different; it is perceived to be the time of the final battle between good and evil.

3. In peacetime, God, or the forces of nature, is not perceived to be particularly involved in human disputes. In wartime, such slogans as "Gott Mit Uns," "In God We Trust," or "Dieu et Mon Droit" express our belief in God's benign protection.

4. In peacetime, the attitude is generally that the future will more or less proceed much as it has in the past. In wartime, the attitude is that if the war is won, things will be much better, but if lost, calamitous. The meaning of the past and the shape of the future hang in a critical balance.

5. In peacetime, life is essentially complex. In wartime, it is simple, with only one focus: victory.

---

[33] LeShan, *The Psychology of War*, 43 .

6. In peacetime, problems exist at many different levels and in many different contexts. In wartime, the issue is typically an act, or acts, of hostility on the part of the enemy that has to be challenged.
7. In peacetime, we search for the cause or causes of a problem. In wartime, we are concerned only with the outcome.
8. In peacetime, people around the world are seen as fundamentally the same. In wartime, they and we are fundamentally different; we are good and they are evil.[34]

It is LeShan's opinion that with the advent of war or the serious threat of war, a shift in the collective perception of reality takes place and the mundane world is abandoned while the mythic world is enthusiastically embraced. It is then that we are psychologically capable of transforming our enemy from fellow human beings into images of the demonic. In so doing, we reduce them to something less than human and are able to kill them and their kind (women and children) without addressing the compelling moral questions that such behavior would normally require.[35]

LeShan is not the first scholar to investigate the enigmatic and volatile behavior of human groups. In the nineteenth century, Gustave Le Bon, a French social psychologist, published his classic *The Crowd,* in which he argued that in a particular context, individual consciousness could be submerged and dominated by the collective mind of the crowd. It was his observation that when a number of people are gathered together for purposes of action, new psychological characteristics emerge that are different from those of the individuals who compose

---

[34] LeShan, *The Psychology of War,* 34–35.
[35] LeShan, *The Psychology of War,* 37.

the group. It is as though an individual's conscious personality suddenly vanishes while a collective personality appears in its stead. Beneath the weight of predisposing influences—a national crisis for instance—and under the sway of a charismatic leader, profound emotions can be evoked. Importantly, in a crowd, an individual can give way to the power of suggestion and under its influence his or her critical thinking can be compromised.[36]

As part of the crowd, Le Bon contended, an individual acquires a sense of invincible power by reason of the large number of persons involved at the same time that his or her sense of personal responsibility is lessened. In a crowd, emotions and actions can be contagious and the individual can be moved to suppress personal interests for a perceived greater good, even to the point of sacrificing life itself.

In summary, Le Bon characterized crowd behavior as the submergence of the individual conscious mind and the emergence of a predominantly unconscious crowd mentality. The charismatic leader, moreover, possessing the power of suggestion, can direct certain feelings and ideas toward a single purpose and can skillfully transform the crowd's sentiments into action; a rational individual can be readily induced to embrace violence or other behaviors that can descend ultimately into acts of barbarism.[37] Reports of the abuse and torture of Iraqi prisoners by American personnel at Abu Ghraib prison in Baghdad, for instance, represent the most recent example of the deplorable consequences resulting from this powerful but generally ignored psychological phenomenon.

---

[36] Gustave Le Bon, *The Crowd: A Study of the Popular Mind* (Atlanta: Cherokee, 1982), chap. 1.

[37] Le Bon, *The Crowd*, 9–12

Half a century ago, Robert E. Conot published his monumental report *Justice at Nuremberg,* which documented the heinous acts that ordinary German citizens perpetrated against their perceived enemies on behalf of the Third Reich.[38] Both Hanna Arendt in her book *Eichmann in Jerusalem: A Report on the Banality of Evil*[39] and Robert J. Lifton in his landmark study *Nazi Doctors: Medical Killing and the Psychology of Genocide* observed how ordinary their subjects were and how commonplace—banal—their responses were to their interrogator's questions about their willing complicity in one of humankinds darkest periods.[40]

These two studies complement the work of the psychologists LeShan and Le Bon, as well as Lifton's earlier pioneering study in 1954 of the Chinese communist government's program to reform and re-educate political dissidents. Lifton's analysis of the technique of what now is called brainwashing permits us to understand more clearly how the judgment and autonomy of a person can also be profoundly compromised through conscious manipulation.[41]

The American psychologist Stanley Milgram, in his book *Obedience to Authority,* examined how the average person could readily engage in acts of cruelty toward fellow humans. His analysis drew upon the results of a study involving several hundred volunteers from a cross-section of the U.S. population. Milgram informed the participants simply that in "the interest of

---

[38] Robert E. Conot, *Justice at Nuremberg* (New York: Carroll and Graf, 1983).

[39] Hanna Arendt, *Eichmann in Jerusalem: A Report on the Banality of Evil* (New York: Penguin Books, 1994).

[40] Robert J. Lifton, *Nazi Doctors: Medical Killing and the Psychology of Genocide* (New York: Basic Books, 1986).

[41] Robert J. Lifton, *Thought Reform and the Psychology of Totalism: A Study of Brainwashing in China* (Chapel Hill: University of North Carolina Press, 1989).

advancing science" they were to administer electric shocks of increasing voltage to a fellow subject. Despite the pleadings by the subject to stop the shocks (who in fact received no shocks at all but was instructed to express degrees of pain and distress), the participants continued to administer the presumed electric shocks to the maximum demanded by the instructor—a maximum that was clearly labeled "Danger: Severe Shock."[42]

Milgram interprets the results of his obedience experiments by arguing that human beings live within hierarchical structures and that we can easily be seduced by the trappings of authority that can control our perceptions and behaviors. He proposes that since human beings live in such hierarchical groupings—which from an evolutionary perspective provide an enormous advantage over the isolated individual in coping with the challenges of existence—submission to authority helps to explain why otherwise normal people will perform extreme misanthropic acts when directed.[43]

Milgram's research gives added credence to the work of LeShan, Le Bon, and Lifton concerning the persuasive power of the group and the role of authority in social life.

In summary, the combined research on obedience and thought control suggests that an individual can not only submit to the will of the group under what might be called natural conditions, but he or she can also be artificially induced to forgo established personal beliefs and cherished principles.

What can we conclude from this brief review of the proposed causes of war? Simply put: human aggression—which, it has been theorized, can be found in our biological nature, social institutions, individual or crowd psychology, or the Will of

---

[42] Stanley Milgram, *Obedience to Authority* (New York: Harper Perennial, 1983), chap. 1.

[43] Milgram, *Obedience to Authority*, 123–25.

God—manifests itself in a variety of ways for a variety of reasons. As a result, the age-old search for the cause or causes of war—despite the dedicated and painstaking efforts of countless individuals, representing a diversity of disciplines and interests—has been largely inconclusive.

Given the uncertainty that bedevils us with respect to why human beings are episodically homicidal, it is useful to explore the issue further and ask a different set of questions from those that have been traditionally posed.

For instance, what in war—except for its regular generational eruptions—is constant? What beliefs or practices do we find intrinsic in this time-honored institution that promotes and supports such lethal and destructive behavior? What role does the Judeo-Christian creation myth, in particular with its promise of immortality, play for those who willingly die in defense of their faith?

In addressing these questions, I would argue that it needs to be recognized that war has served to define, even before the Christian era, the male role. The right and privilege to engage in mortal conflict, to display one's courage, loyalty, and selflessness, has been both reserved for and required of the young male. One need only recall the notable feats of the Sumerian king Gilgamesh, the legendary exploits of the Greek hero Ulysses, or the undaunted courage of the boy David in his encounter with the giant Goliath to recognize that to go willingly to war has been the definitive test for establishing one's manhood. As a consequence, war has served as the ultimate experience for defining the status of men. In America, for instance, the Medal of Honor, the Tomb of the Unknown Soldier, Memorial Day, and other honorific symbols, sacred places, and commemorative occasions dramatically express this historic connection between war and masculinity.

War gives life meaning; to die in defense of what one ultimately cherishes—faith, homeland, honor—brings dignity to one's death. It makes life purposeful and one's death comprehendible. Death—heroic death, death willingly embraced—is seen as a far greater thing than to suffer death like a cowering dog or dumbly like a sacrificial animal. In this respect, war, paradoxically, shares with play the important function of releasing humans, if only for a moment, from the iron law of nature or the punishing rod of God. Figuratively, the soldier has death at his command. He brings death up from the earth and down from the sky and in the heroic act of dying, his life is made intelligible. As St. Paul might observe, death has lost its sting. One's death is no longer piacular—an atonement; to the contrary, its peculiarity is reversed. What was once perceived as the wages of sin is now celebratory. The notable monuments, sacred burial sites, commemorative days of mourning, and other occasions and places that pay tribute to the heroic and never-to-be-forgotten sacrifice of the dead are testimony to the importance of the role of war in humankind's endless quest for immortality.

The Judeo-Christian paradigm plays a singular role in war. I have already observed that war can involve different kinds of conflict, express different goals and purposes, and stem from a variety of causes. Regardless of what purpose or motivation is behind the decision to engage in war, there is a theological component to war that needs to be acknowledged.

Since the dawn of Christianity, since God's promise to the Roman emperor Constantine that he would defeat his enemies if he were to do battle under the Christian cross, war in Western culture has come to incorporate the theme that forms the core of the Judeo-Christian creation myth: the salvation of the human soul.

Participation in a justifiable war—a war in defense of one's country—calls for the highest expression of the human spirit. The eloquence of England's prime minister Winston Churchill at the time of the Battle of Britain, for example, continues to resonate through the halls of memory, as does President Roosevelt's call to arms following the day "that will live forever in infamy": December 7, 1941, the day Japan attacked Pearl Harbor. President Roosevelt concluded his declaration of war before the joint Congress of the United States by solemnly intoning: "With confidence in our armed forces—with the unbounded determination of our people—we will gain the inevitable triumph—so help us God."

The heroic act of bravery of bomber pilot Captain Colin Kelly in attacking a Japanese battleship single-handedly, and the endurance and courage of the soldiers and nurses during the Bataan death march are but two of the countless instances that affirmed Roosevelt's tocsin speech that all needed to rise up to their fullest height of courage and dedication in order to confront and overcome an implacable enemy. More recently, President Bush, following the September 11, 2001, destruction of the World Trade Center by al-Qaeda terrorists, addressed the nation on television to express America's defiance. He concluded with the following words of assurance: "The course of this conflict is not known, yet its outcome is certain. Freedom and fear, justice and cruelty, have always been at war, and we know that God is not neutral between them."[44]

Thus, we see in our encounter with war the process by which both society and the individual respond to the prophesies and promises intrinsic to the Judeo-Christian narrative: that through individual sacrifice and collective effort, a nation, under God,

---

[44] George W. Bush, *Address to Joint Session of Congress and the American People* (Washington, DC: September 20, 2001).

will triumph over its enemies while its fallen heroes will triumph over their mortality. In this light, Mardi Gras, discussed earlier, can be viewed as the civilian equivalent to the experience of war to the extent that it embodies the two central issues at the heart of Christianity: the persistence of society through historical time and the survival of the individual through eternity.

Integral to this discussion is the concept of oblivion, the death of the soul. The fear that one faces the threat of being spiritually separated eternally from God is a belief that has hung threateningly over the Christian faithful, like the sword of Damocles, for the past two thousand years. I would argue that the tolerance for war and the willingness to give up one's mortal life in pursuit of it finds justification in the conviction that to die in defense of one's country is redemptive, a belief summed up in the motto "Duty, Country, Honor." Or, as one Christian martyr succinctly expressed it as he awaited his death, "He is no fool who gives up what he cannot keep, to gain what he cannot lose."[45]

---

[45] John Foxe, *Lives of Martyrs* (Peabody, MA: Hendrickson, 2004), xii.

Chapter 8:
Death

We owe God a death.

> —Shakespeare (Henry IV Act III Scene II)

Neither the sun nor death can be looked at with a steady eye.

> —Francois de la Rochefoucauld

Ring around the rosie
Pocket full of posey
Ashes, ashes, all fall down.

> —Children's nursery rhyme

The long habit of living indisposeth us for dying

> —Sir Thomas Browne

Since I was so early done for
I wonder what I was begun for.

> —Epitaph (New England Cemetery)

Do not go gentle into that good night
Rage, rage against the dying of the light.

> —Dylan Thomas

Death is the great rupturer; it is immanent in life and part of the continuous transition in which all organisms grow and decay. Historically, a person has been defined as dead if his or her heart and lungs cease to function or eyes fail to react to light or the body to pain.[1] While the cells of the brain cease functioning within a few minutes after death, surface hair, skin, and bone cells may continue to grow for several hours.

The challenge of determining when death has actually occurred has become increasingly complicated in recent years by advances in medical technology. Procedures now make it possible to define a person as dead whose brain measures no electrical activity (as recorded on an electroencephalogram) for a period of twenty-four hours, even though the heart and lungs may still be functioning through the use of mechanical aides.

The question of exactly when death occurs is crucial for the practice of organ transplant surgery. The traditional definition of death, depending as it did on the heart and the circulation of the blood, constituted a serious obstacle to the successful development of this new technology. The concept of brain death, introduced in the 1960s by Henry Beecher at Harvard

---

[1] In this connection, it should be noted that putrefaction since time immemorial has also been recognized as a sign of death, but modern sensibilities have become so highly developed that this fifth indicator is often left unmentioned as too indelicate for discussion. For example, in an early nineteenth-century edition of the Holy Bible, the account of Christ raising his friend Lazarus from the dead describes the condition of Lazarus's body as "he stinketh." A century or so later, the editors of the new Holy Bible, Revised Standard Version, replaced that sentence with "there will be an odor" but by 1970, the editors of the Jerusalem Bible had again changed the text to read "by now he will smell." These changes in the biblical text are consistent with Elias's aforementioned observations concerning the direction of the civility curve in Western society.

and now adopted universally, states that death occurs when the brain is dead, not whether there is a heartbeat.[2] Such a definition permits the maintenance of the circulatory system until the organs are removed without the implication that they were removed from a still-living individual.

The establishment of this new definition of death marks a new stage in humankind's age-old struggle with the Damoclean threat of mortality. Over the millennia, we have not only sought to find the various causes of death and its prevention, but we have also labored to understand its meaning. Within the historic Christian tradition, the ontological question "Why must I die?" has been explained as a consequence of humankind's fall from grace. According to this belief, death, no less than life, is an expression of divine will. Death is a unique issue between God and His creation and its very purposefulness places humankind at the very center of existence. In II Corinthians 4:10–11, we read, "We, which live are always delivered unto death for Jesus' sake, that the life also of Jesus might be made manifest in our mortal flesh." Death, the scriptures declare, is the gateway to immortality and part of the divine plan. Shakespeare echoes this obligation for humans to die when, in Henry IV, he says simply, "We owe God a death." In the Christian tradition, death is the prerequisite for life in this world, as well as in the life to come.

Henry Ford Sr., founder of the Ford Motor Company, probably embodied the essence of the American spirit more completely than anyone else. Aldous Huxley acknowledged this in his novel *Brave New World* when he proposed that Americans calculate time not according to the year of Our Lord but according to the year of our Ford.[3] What Huxley meant by this astute remark was that Ford brought into the twentieth century

---

[2] Henry Beecher, *Contemporary Issues in Bioethics* (1982): 288–93.
[3] Aldous Huxley, *Brave New World* (New York: Harper, 1998), 20.

new principles of industrial organization. In doing so, Ford was singularly instrumental in transforming America from an agrarian to an industrial society, and from a rural to an urban-centered way of life. As a consequence, he profoundly changed the conditions of our world as well as our ideas and beliefs concerning it.

Only a few generations ago Americans lived much as the ancient Greeks and Romans once did; great numbers of people were compelled to go to the fields and forests, or the lakes and rivers, for their livelihood. They lived by the dictates of nature and chance as well as by the belief in divine intervention. There were always the questions of where tomorrow's meal would come from, whether a child would be born alive, whether a cow would calve, or whether fire or drought or other natural calamity would destroy the work of an individual, a family, a community, or a generation. The subsequent increased control over our lives and environment that Ford's path-breaking efforts provided greatly changed the conditions of our fragile existence and in so doing, reduced our dependency on, as well as fear of, nature.

One important change brought about by the industrialization and urbanization of America was how we dealt with death. Families began to give up their traditional responsibility for the care and disposition of a deceased family member and turn the task over to a paid functionary—the mortician. I do not mean to suggest that there were no morticians or undertakers before the time of Henry Ford. In Egypt, Asia, and Europe—essentially everywhere—there have always been those who have assisted in laying out the dead and disposing of a corpse. In colonial America, for instance, the task was frequently given over to a nurse-midwife following the untimely death of a mother or her child. The general practice of releasing a body to a funerary specialist, however, was first introduced in the United States around the time of the Civil War, fostered by the war's high death toll and the introduction of embalming. Additionally, the newly developed network of railroads allowed the dead to be returned home for burial.

By the time of World War I, the decline of the custom of a family being responsible for the disposition of their dead was furthered by the movement of families and individuals from rural areas to cities and towns across the country in search of employment. As a result, people began to live more separate and private lives. The combination of the separation of relatives and friends, the rush and complexity of city life, and the time-oriented character of the new industrial order compelled families to assign the heretofore private task of laying out and burying their dead to a public functionary.

Between World War I and the end of World War II, many of Ford's industrial principles and practices were adopted by other occupations and professions. The exigencies of war put such a demand on medical resources that the all-inclusive public hospital became a necessity. It was no longer efficient or economically practical for a physician to make house calls. Hospitals offered what the individual practitioner could not: specialists in a variety of fields, a nursing staff, modern medical equipment, blood banks, and a hygienic environment. People went to the hospital. Today, it is estimated that more than six persons out of ten who will die in the United States in any given year will do so in some type of medical facility. [4]

Thus we can observe the culmination of a process whereby, within the space of a century, the dead are removed from the home, the seriously and chronically ill are removed to the hospital; and, increasingly, the elderly are assigned to nursing

---

[4] "End of Life Issues and Care: Historical Changes Affecting End-of-Life Care." *APA Online*, February 8, 2006 http://www.apa.org/pi/eol/historical.html.

homes or assisted-care facilities, all under the supervision of paid specialists.

The aging of American society has cast a new light not only on the aging process itself and its problems but also on the issue of mortality. In the United States, millions of citizens now find themselves in advanced middle age. This modern development has made the subject of death—a topic generally avoided—open to public discussion and to medical and scholarly concern.

And so it should. Interest in the subject of death in the United States has been driven in large measure over the past fifty years by the simple demographic fact that the population is aging. During the twentieth century, while the number of people younger than age sixty-five tripled, the number of people older than age sixty-five increased by a factor of eleven. In 2005, 12 percent of the population was over sixty-five years of age.[5] In 1995, those aged between sixty-five and seventy-four (18.8 million people) represented an age group eight times larger than in 1900; those aged seventy-five to eighty-four were fourteen times larger as a group, while those eighty-five years of age and older were twenty-nine times as large an age group than at the turn of the century.[6] Persons older than age eighty-five now make up the most rapidly growing age group.[7] In 2004, those persons over age eighty-five represented 1.3 percent of the population.[8]

---

[5] Data Finder, Population Reference Bureau, 2005. http://www.prb.org/.

[6] "Demographics-National," Eastern Nebraska Office on Aging 1996, http://www.enoa.org/demographics/index.html.

[7] "Report on Aging in America Outlines Demographic Shifts," *Elder Law Issues* 13, no. 38 (March 20, 2006), http://elder-law.com/2006/Issue1338.html.

[8] "Data on Age," U.S. Census Bureau 2004, May 18, 2006, www.factfinder.census.gov.

American citizens, it is clear, are living longer. In 1776, life expectancy at birth was approximately thirty-five years; in 1900, forty-seven years; in 1950, sixty-eight years; and in the year 2005, seventy-five, with life expectancy slightly higher for women (eighty years) than for men (seventy-five years).[9]

The upshot of this unprecedented demographic transformation in life expectancy is that more people will live long enough to experience multiple chronic illnesses, disability, and dependency. Thus, it has come about that adult children (who are themselves in their fifties and sixties) are those to whom very elderly parents will turn, increasingly, for care. The parent–support ratio illustrates this. This ratio reflects the number of persons older than age eighty-five per 100 persons between the ages of fifty and sixty-four. From 1950 to 1993, the ratio almost tripled from three to ten. Importantly, it is predicted that over the next six decades, the ratio will reach twenty-nine.[10]

American society, at the same time, faces an overall decline in its birthrate, while it continues to experience high residential mobility. In 2003, it is reported that 14 percent of the population changed its place of residence in the United States.[11]

These and other trends, such as the continued growth of retirement communities in Sunbelt states and the ubiquitous spread of nursing homes across the country, serve not only to change the nature of the problems associated with aging, dying,

---

[9] Population Reference Bureau, 2005, http://www.prb.org/.

[10] "End of Life Issues and Care: Historical Changes Affecting End-of-Life Care." *APA Online*, February 8, 2006, http://www.apa.org/pi/eol/historical.html

[11] Mike Bergman, "Moving Rates Lowest in 50+ Years, Census Bureau Reports," March 23, 2004, http://www.census.gov/Press Release/www/releases/archives/mobility_of_the_population/001729.html.

and death but also have the potential to aggravate them. The long-term implications of these isolating and segregating developments can be better understood, however, if we look at other changes that have been taking place in American society.

Family relations have been directly affected by the new social patterns that have emerged. The American family has been transformed both in structure and in type as today's headlines and judicial decisions attest. It is more mobile, socially as well as geographically, than ever before. Today's family can be characterized as primarily child oriented, more democratic than paternalistic, and more individualized than integrated. Moreover, the young contemporary family is no longer a part of a rural community but increasingly resides in a more impersonal, urban environment. In the modern-day metropolis, large numbers of the elderly are retired from work and free of parental and other social obligations. They are often absent from or marginal to the main current of family life. The extension of medical services and the advances in medical science research, moreover, make possible not only the prolongation of their lives but also cause those who are hospitalized for varying periods of time to be separated further from their families and friends. Not the least consequence of these developments is the fact that great numbers of the elderly not only live alone but the prospect is that they will die alone.

These social and demographic shifts are reflected not only in the tenor and tone of the theological debates that have emerged over the past decades regarding life and death issues but also in the change in the public's attitude toward the traditional American funeral.[12] In a society in which only half of the adult

---

[12] L. E. Bowman, *The American Funeral: A Study in Guilt, Extravagance, and Sublimity* (Washington, DC: Public Affairs Press, 1959). See also R. Harmer, *The High Cost of Dying* (New York: Crowell-Collier Press, 1963)

population is church affiliated and in which the social and spatial mobility of its citizens are among its distinguishing features, the religious, emotional, and economic obligations that a funeral imposes on a family have come to be seen by many as burdensome and inappropriate.

Characteristically, the contemporary funeral is for that member of the family least functionally relevant to it. As the anthropologist Jack Goody has observed, "Funerals [in America] today have so much less work to do."[13] Advocacy of memorial services, with the body absent and medical donation of the body or its parts, are attempts within the context of modern, urban society to resolve the different problems associated with the disposition of the dead. Other attempts to contain or limit the social impact of death upon the family or community can be seen in the decline in public obituaries, the dramatic increase in immediate disposition or cremation of the body, the formalization of rules governing employee's bereavement time, and the imposition of stricter Federal Trade Commission guidelines for the funeral industry.[14,15]

The unprecedented developments in the demographic profile of the nation since the end of World War II have caught the attention of gerontologists, demographers, and other concerned scholars. What has been observed over the past six decades in response to these singularly demographic shifts has not only

---

and Jessica Mitford, *The American Way of Death* (New York: Simon and Schuster, 1963).

[13] Jack Goody, "Death and the Interpretation of Culture," in *Death in America*, ed. D. E. Standard (Philadelphia: University of Pennsylvania Press, 1974), 7.

[14] L. Pratt, "Business Temporal Norms and Bereavement Behavior." *American Sociological Review* 46 (1981): 317–33.

[15] "Funeral Industry Practices, Final Staff Report on the Federal Trade Commission and Proposed Trade Regulation Rule" (16 CFR Part 453).

been the increase in the number of facilities for assisted living but also the emergence of hospice care, the ubiquitous growth of secularly based grief counseling programs, and dramatic changes in American funeral practices. In a strikingly short period of time, funeral accoutrements and apparel that traditionally had served to announce a death or express grief and mourning, such as the funeral wreath, widow's weeds, the black hat, black armband and tie, as well as the black-edged letter announcing a death, have virtually disappeared from the American scene. On the other hand, private funerals, tombstone-free memorial parks and nondenominational disposal services have proliferated.

More than seventy years ago, the sociologist Thomas Eliot called for an objective, secular study of death.[16] While anthropologists had examined the burial rites and funeral customs of preliterate or nonindustrial peoples, and social workers had addressed the social and economic issues surrounding widowhood, medical and social science researchers in the United States were virtually silent on the subject. For the most part, death was seen as an unfathomable subject not suitable for scientific research and best left to the clergy and theologians. There were, of course, exceptions. As early as 1915 the distinguished psychologist G. Stanley Hall addressed the subject in his classic essay "Thanatophobia and Immortality."[17] Throughout the succeeding decades, psychologists such as W. Bromberg,[18] P. Schilder,[19] F. Deutsch,[20] W. C. Middleton,[21] and

---

[16] T. D. Eliot, "The Adjusted Behavior of Bereaved Families: A New Field of Research," *Social Forces* 8 (1930): 543–49.

[17] G. Stanley Hall, "Thanatophobia and Immortality," *American Journal of Psychology* 26 (1915): 550–613.

[18] Walter Bromberg, "Death and Dying," *Psychoanalytic Review* 20 (1933): 133–85.

R. May[22] explored such topics as death symbols, attitudes toward death among children, the relationship between religious beliefs and death, death anxiety, and euthanasia. Still, little was known in an objective, scientific way about the impact of death and its sequelae upon the individual or society.

It was not until the early 1940s, when the psychiatrist Eric Lindemann of Harvard University investigated the reactions of the survivors of the Coconut Grove fire (a Boston nightclub that burned in 1941 with the loss of over 500 young lives), that this situation changed. Lindemann's classic report, "Symptomatology and Management of Acute Grief," dramatically highlighted the medical, psychological, and sociological significance of the event. His historic study of grief was brought into still sharper focus by the studies of Anna Freud and her colleagues on the separation of English schoolchildren from their families during the Second World War.[23]

For the most part, these studies and observations were restricted to a limited academic audience. It was the psychologist Herman Feifel who, in 1959, with the publication of his path-breaking compendium *The Meaning of Death*, brought the discussion of death out of the halls of academe and into the

---

[19] P. Schilder, "The Attitude of Murderers toward Death," *Journal of Abnormal and Social Psychology* 31 (1936): 348–63.

[20] F. Deutsch, "Absence of Grief," *Psychoanalytic Quarterly* 6 (1937): 12–22.

[21] W. C. Middleton, "Some Reactions toward Death among College Students," *Journal of Abnormal and Social Psychology* 31 (1936): 165–73.

[22] R. May, *The Meaning of Anxiety* (New York: Ronald Press, 1950).

[23] E. Lindemann, "Symptomatology and Management of Acute Grief," *American Journal of Psychiatry* 101 (1944): 141–48.

public forum.[24] The process by which Feifel accomplished this, however, was, as he has wryly observed, "not an easy birth."[25]

In 1958, Feifel proposed to survey first-year medical students regarding their attitudes toward dying and death. The study never saw the light of day because he was refused access to the students on the grounds that the interviews would distress them. At that time, the ward that accommodated dying patients was not only segregated but was referred to as the "catastrophic" ward and restricted to senior medical students. This was the operative word employed by the hospital administrator, even though it was fifteen years after World War II, and the word *catastrophic* had taken on a more momentous connotation.

Since the publication of *The Meaning of Death*, studies of grief and the exploration of attitudes toward death appeared increasingly in social and medical science literature. It is of interest to note that more material by professional scholars and researchers was published on the subject of death, grief, and bereavement within five years following the release of Feifel's book than had appeared over the previous century.

This is not to say that humankind has not taken note of the problems associated with death throughout the course of history. To the contrary; in both the sacred and profane literature of Western culture can be found references to the meaning and significance of dying and death, as well as to the profound experience of grief. The Roman orator Cicero, for instance, instructs us that "There is no grief that time does not lessen or soften,"[26] and in John 11:35 we learn that "Jesus wept" upon hearing of the death of his friend Lazarus. Shakespeare has

---

[24] H. Feifel, ed., *The Meaning of Death* (New York: McGraw-Hill, 1959).

[25] H. Feifel, "Death," in *Taboo Topics*, ed. N. Farberow (New York: Atherton, 1963), 8.

[26] Cicero, *Epistolae*, act IV, scene v. in *Dictionary of Quotations*, Bergan Evans, ed., (New York, Bonanza Books 1968), 292.

Brabantio in *Othello* cry, "my particular grief is of so flood-gate and o'er bearing nature that it engluts and swallows other sorrows,"[27] and in *Macbeth*, Shakespeare instructs us to "Give sorrow words; the grief that does not speak whispers the o'er-fraught heart and bids it break."[28] Victor Hugo in *Les Miserables* observed that "Great grief is a divine and terrible radiance which transfigures the wretched."[29] But it is Shakespeare who has the last word when he reminds us shrewdly that "everyone can master a grief but he that has it." Over the centuries, humankind has paid attention. We have observed in our bereavements the many faces of grief. Yet it must be said that the literary and philosophical observations—to say nothing of the extensive religious literature, *Ars Moriendi* (the art of dying)—did not provide us with a systematic clinical knowledge regarding the social or emotional experience of dying, nor enlighten us overly about the sociological or psychological elements of loss and grief.

Death avoidance in the years after World War II is understandable. The war was cataclysmic. It was an event of unprecedented magnitude that eclipsed even the suffering and devastation of World War I, claiming more than 52 million lives worldwide. It resulted in the destruction or damage to thousands of cities, towns, and villages across the world, left millions of men, women, and children without food or shelter, and millions more as refugees. A kaleidoscope of images from that time readily comes to mind: London in flames, the devastation of Pearl Harbor, the gaunt and exhausted face of a

---

[27] William Shakespeare, *Othello*, act I, scene iii. in *Dictionary of Quotations*, Bergan Evans, ed., (New York, Bonanza Books 1968), 292.

[28] William Shakespeare, *Macbeth*, act IV, scene iii. in *Dictionary of Quotations*, Bergan Evans, ed., (New York, Bonanza Books 1968), 293.

[29] Victor Hugo, *Les Miserables*, act V, Scene xiii. in *Dictionary of Quotations*, Bergan Evans, ed., (New York, Bonanza Books 1968), 293.

young soldier, the hauntingly bleak landscape of Hiroshima, Auschwitz. The American public recoiled from such apocalyptic visions and, psychologically, turned away.

Other factors and social trends, less dramatic and slower in their effect than the war, played a part in our coming to shy away from the subject of death. Improved public health and medical services led to a significant decline in infant mortality at the same time that they gave rise to an increase in the birth rate and longevity.

One of the more questionable responses that emerged from the brute fact of death in recent years is the cryogenic movement, first proposed in the 1960s by Robert Ettinger. He promoted the idea that if one could be frozen following death then at some future time, as advances in medical technology allowed, the deceased could be thawed and restored to life. Although few persons over the succeeding decades have agreed to participate in such a questionable venture, it should be noted that Ted Williams, an icon of American baseball, recently had his head refrigerated in anticipation of just such a prospect.[30] More recently, a society calling itself the World Transhumanist Association, which boasts a membership of 3,000 in twenty-four chapters across ninety-eight countries, is also interested in life extension, including the possibility of immortality. It is their opinion that the emerging science of molecular machines (nanotechnology) rather than the dubious practice of freezing a corpse will someday repair our bodies from the inside out and transform us into a new species. Genetic engineering, artificial joints, cochlear implants, and mood-altering and memory-enhancing drugs represent just the beginning of a time, they claim, when we will be able to enhance our brains, improve our

---

[30] "Please Don't Call the Customers Dead," *New York Times*, February 13, 2005.

bodies, and possibly live forever. In the meantime, it has long been reported that a health spa in Mexico serves a cocktail mix that includes the first bowel movement of a newborn child as part of a breakfast menu for those clients who, in the grand tradition of Ponce de Leon, wish to remain forever young.

A custom alluded to earlier that has emerged in contemporary society, and that has had the effect of veiling the dying and death of our aged members in a more immediate way, is the practice of citizens of northern states relocating to southern states at the time of their retirement. The migration of large numbers of elderly persons from the Snowbelt to the Sunbelt, even for part of the year, encourages the separation of those most likely to die from their family and friends. Such a development in modern life permits us to minimize our encounter with death and potentially mute the grief and anguish of bereavement. Time and separation loosen family and friendship ties. Once an older person is physically or geographically separated from his or her family, the person's death can, potentially, register less heavily upon it.

I think it is fair to say that from the end of World War I until the late 1950s, death in America, in a manner of speaking, took a holiday. Paradoxically, the public discussion of death—despite its ubiquitous and oftentimes dramatic appearance—was for the most part, meager or muted and almost always euphemistic. Death was considered such an omnipotent omnipresence, something beyond all human understanding, that it was not readily discussed. Indeed, it was considered impolite to talk about death; to utter the word threatened to evoke its presence.

Louise Pound, an English professor at the University of Nebraska early in the 1930s, was intrigued by the nation's squeamishness in the face of mortality. She subsequently compiled a list of more than 370 euphemistic expressions that served to avoid the straightforward mention of the word death in everyday discourse. Every ingenuity, she reported, was employed to shroud death's ultimate reality. The greatest number of euphemisms she found were sentimental or poetic with the purpose of evoking gentle emotions or identifying death with a romantic melancholy or gracious dignity. Among the literary and figurative expressions that she gathered were such evasions as "laid down his burden," "called home," "gathered to his fathers," "released from the burden of the weary world," "is with the angels," "called to his final reward," "called to God, " called to Jesus," and "gave up the ghost."[31]

She found that metaphors of sleep and rest were also prominent in deflecting the reality of death. Among her examples from this category are "called to heavenly rest," "laid to rest," "rest in peace," "called to the eternal sleep," and "safe in the arms of Jesus," while for metaphors of departure, she cited, "passed on/away/over," "gone home," "gone to his heavenly home," "gone to glory," "passed to his reward," "gone to his fathers," and "gone to meet his maker."

Dr. Pound reported that flippant and slang expressions alluding to death enjoyed a certain popularity among all sections of the population and were characterized by humor, vulgarity, and a general spirit of defiance. Such examples included "kick the bucket," "pushing up the daisies," "gone to pot," "shuffled off," "gone home in a box," "croaked," "is counting the worms," and "knocked off."

Metaphors from work and recreation also found their place on her extensive list, while those related to war comprised a significant portion of the catalogue. They included "bit the bullet," "fired his last shot," "went to answer the last roll call,"

---

[31] Louise Pound, "American Euphemisms for Dying, Death and Burial," *American Speech* 11(1936): 195–202.

"gave up the ship," "went to Davy Jones' locker," "checked out," and "went to the last roundup."

Dr. Pound suggested that the miscellaneous euphemisms surrounding the material adjuncts of death, such as the coffin or the cemetery, were even more necessary in order to avoid a forthright mention of such concrete evidence of death. She perceptively observed that their elaborateness was evidence of the strength of the taboo. Metaphors for the dead included "the departed," "the deceased," and "the late lamented"; for the coffin, "the casket," "the wooden overcoat," "the wooden kimono," and "the eternity box"; while for the cemetery, she recorded such euphemisms as "the marble orchard," "the bone yard," "memorial park," and "Hell's half acre."

She commented that it is as difficult to prophesize a death as it is to announce it, and the same impulse to disguise one's meaning that gives rise to the euphemism could be found in the attempt to evade it as an accomplished fact or an inevitable outcome. Her list in this category of euphemisms included "your number is up," "you are on your last legs," "You're under sailing orders," "You'll be sent home in a box," and "Step softly, kind friend, for you, too, will meet your end."

While a generation of Americans have lived and died since Dr. Pound published her informative research, the desire to avoid the fact of our mortality still remains, even if the manner of its disguise is transformed—*plus ça change, plus c'est la même chose.*

A striking example of the avoidance that surrounded death within the academic community during this period can be found in the four-volume social science survey entitled *The American Soldier.*[32] This prodigious project examined the attitudes and

---

[32] S. Stouffer et al., *The American Soldier* (Princeton: Princeton University Press, 1949).

reactions of more than two million soldiers concerning their World War II experiences and helped to establish the basis for the Point Four Program that determined which military personnel, and in what order, would be returned home from active duty following the war's cessation. The social science researchers asked a comprehensive series of questions on a diverse range of topics but, markedly, failed to ask a single question about a soldier's experiences with, or fear of, death.

It had not always been so. When I was a boy I was taken along with our entire fifth grade class to the home of a classmate who had died of scarlet fever. She was laid out on a couch in the living room and we were all ushered by her body to pay our respects. While it was the first time that most of us had ever seen a human corpse, I don't recall that it was traumatic; I remember, if anything, a sense of restrained excitement. In those days as children, if we did not witness our mother wringing or cutting off the head of a chicken or goose for a holiday meal, we would have occasionally seen a dead horse or other animal lying on a road or in a field. Times were simpler then, and we lived with animals in a way that today has largely vanished. Moreover, our classroom textbooks addressed the fact of death, especially the death of children, in a manner that was unthinkable in the period following World War II. In a popular textbook of the time, *The McGuffey Reader,* more than 10 percent of its content addressed the subject of loss and grief during its extended use in American classrooms.

At the turn of the century, children under the age of fifteen accounted for the majority of all deaths (54 percent). They died from such contagious and infectious diseases as smallpox, scarlet fever, diphtheria, diarrhea, tuberculosis, and pneumonia. Today, the leading causes of death are cancer, heart attacks, and stroke—primarily afflictions of the elderly—who now constitute approximately three quarters of the persons who die in any one year in the United States.[33]

It is important to observe that not only has there been a significant change in our proximity to death in modern society, but a profound shift has also occurred in our general attitude toward death. Increasingly, death is no longer viewed as the result of divine displeasure or the price of moral trespass. For many, death is not perceived in the Judeo-Christian view as "the wages of sin." Rather, death has come to be seen as the result of personal negligence or an unforeseen accident and viewed increasingly as a temporal matter that we treat much as we would an avoidable illness. Like some noxious disease, it is a personal embarrassment to be discussed only reluctantly with one's physician. Despite recent educational efforts to the contrary and increased media attention, death continues to be a proscribed topic in America. It is still a subject of considerable avoidance and denial even if, paradoxically, it can be the focus for public entertainment or on occasion rise to the level of a public spectacle.

The significance of the mass media in both depicting our modern attitude toward death as well as describing our contemporary responses to it cannot be minimized. If we look for a moment at how films addressed the topic of death in the past, compared with today, we can perhaps catch something of the nature and significance of this transition.

The early film classic *Dracula*, for example, clearly delineated the traditional polarity of good and evil envisioned by Christian theology. Within the dramatic structure of the film, Dracula is portrayed as the personification of evil who seduces his hapless victims so as to cause them spiritual death. Only the symbols of

---

[33] Nadine R. Sahyoun, "Trends and Causes of Death among the Elderly," www.cdc.gov 2001.

the Christian God—light, holy water, and the crucifix—can prevail against Dracula, while the tree of life, symbolically transformed into a wooden stake, rids us of his spiritual threat when driven through his heart.

The struggle between good and evil can be seen in our traditional western films with great clarity. In movies such as *High Noon*, the protagonist is a virtuous and courageous God-fearing man who is typically confronted with evil in the form of cattle-rustlers, claim-jumpers, or other scofflaws. Without compromise, the hero rights wrong, restores the law, and reaffirms the moral order. Today, such a perspective is challenged by a profoundly different worldview—relativistic secularism.

The image of modern existential man portrayed today on the screen, epitomized by such characters as James Bond, is that of a handsome, virile, and intelligent young man who functions easily within his environment but who is not necessarily a part of it. His values are both relative and pragmatic, and as amorphous as are those with whom he struggles. He works on behalf of an organization as little known to him and possibly as hostile toward him as are his unknown adversaries. For a cause that transcends his individual self, our modern antihero considers himself expendable, as are those with whom he competes. His attachment to life—a life abundant with power, wealth, and sexual gratification—is made existentially dramatic by the fact that at any given moment he may be compelled to give it up. Carelessness or expediency may cause him to receive a fatal thrust from an enemy or a deadly blow from a friend. Life for our contemporary protagonist in such a world is immediate, sensual, relative, and solitary, while his death is irrelevant. In contrast to our traditional conception of one's social existence, this emerging utilitarian vision of self may well augur a new social order.

Contemporary films, moreover, are explicit in showing violent death of, and by, the young. In recent years such films as *Straw Dogs, The Texas Chainsaw Massacre, Friday the 13th, Nightmare on Elm Street, The Night of the Living Dead, The Terminator, Silence of the Lambs,* and *Saw* have depicted, in color and sometimes in slow motion, the bizarre destruction of human beings that eclipse the meaning of the death itself.

Death's presence in the media is simultaneously everywhere, at once illusively fantastical and frighteningly real. It is the dramatically visceral experience of the collapse of the World Trade Center with its thousands of tragic deaths; the witnessing of an attempted assassination of a pope; an interview with Stephen King promoting his most recent horror novel; a ten-second radio commercial for cemetery plots; the television series *Buffy the Vampire Slayer* in which a young woman is perpetually obliged to kill someone, or the funeral home drama *Six Feet Under,* in which death—sans teeth—is brought sprightly into the living rooms of America; a report of an act of terrorism in some part of the world or a detailed account of multiple homicides in one's hometown; an image of a child with a swollen belly dying of AIDS in Africa, or the sheet-draped body of a young suicide victim.

While prime-time television features death and violence relentlessly, particularly among the young, it portrays grief and the ruptured lives that death can leave in its wake superficially. Television news programs characteristically submerge the human meaning of death at the same time they depersonalize the event by sandwiching reports of loss of life between advertisements or mundane news items.

Death and acts of violence find contemporary expression in other art forms. Francis Bacon, the English expressionist, and his colleague, the painter Acconci, both of whom have paintings on display in the Museum of Modern Art, feature works that depict, in vivid detail, acts of annihilation and mutilation, while the French artist Jacques Tingueley is known for his mechanical constructions that self-destruct as part of their presentation.

Popular music directed at youth contains a morbid fascination with death. Only a few years ago, teenagers flocked to rock concerts to hear Alice Cooper sing, "I Love the Dead," while he assaulted a female mannequin or beheaded a likeness of himself. A survey of themes of death in popular music has shown that death's catastrophic and destructive elements are dramatized or viewed as interference with one's life, rather than acknowledged as a natural part of human existence.[34]

Death, as we have long come to know with the works of such popular fabulists as Agatha Christie, Dashiell Hammett, Arthur Conan Doyle, and Stephen King, is a staple theme in popular fiction. Murder mysteries and espionage thrillers compete to devise ever more titillating and ingenious methods of killing a victim. In recent years with the emergence of a new sci-fi, high-tech horror literature, such competition has become even more intense. A notable example of this genre is *Brain* by Robin Cook. In this best-selling thriller, Cook brings the book to climax with the image of five nude women floating in large, liquid-filled glass cases. Skull-less and faceless but artificially alive, their brains are hooked up to a battery of computers. These living corpses are encouraged to participate in scientific experiments through the stimulation of the sensual areas of their brains. As a reward for their participation, they experience an orgasm a hundred times more powerful than normal. This

---

[34] Kimara Elaine Krief Winters, An Electronic Book of the Dead: A Critical Analysis of Death and Grief in Contemporary American Television Drama, unpublished MA thesis, University of Minnesota, 1995.

necrophilic fantasy concludes with the corpses pleading repeatedly, "Stimulate me, please."[35]

Death in the everyday world, however, differs significantly from death in the media both in terms of cause as well as consequence. Most actual deaths, as I have observed, involve elderly persons who die in hospitals from such illnesses as heart disease, cancer, or stroke. Television or movie fare, as well as the death-inspired genre of literature and music, on the other hand, would lead one to believe that a typical death is violent and characteristically the experience of the young.[36]

The experience of dying is often profound, and a death can result in inconsolable grief. Personal and social readjustment in the face of such loss can be both painful and difficult. Although these aspects of death have traditionally been a major theme and inspiration for much of the world's great art, literature, and music, they are markedly missing as a subject of interest or concern in the popular media. More typically, the media treat death casually and impersonally and sometimes humorously and irreverently, while ignoring its human significance.

What sense can we make out of this fascination with macabre death that has cut a deep swath across popular culture and, like the Pied Piper, has captured the attention of American youth?

Franz Borkenau, the late German historian, was one of the first scholars to recognize that new definitions of the social self and the social order were emerging. He characterized the modern era as post-Christian and argued that with the disintegration of the belief in immortality, modern society was prepared to embrace a nihilistic philosophy of despair and denial. Borkenau believed that secularism would ultimately deny the relevance of selfhood so that death, finally, would be

---

[35] Robin Cooke, *Brain* (New York: Signet. 1999), 288.
[36] Winters, An Electronic Book of the Dead, 90.

"defeated"; that is, it would have no social consequence. It was Borkenau's conviction that to avoid existential extinction, the individual would find a sense of identity through some temporal absolute such as a racial, social, or national group. The film character of James Bond, it could be contended, is the cinematic image of Borkenau's vision of nihilistic man.[37]

It is Borkenau's provocative theory that the shift in our attitudes toward death is traceable to the conflicting attitudes toward death experienced by the unconscious.[38] Briefly, his psychoanalytical-informed view of history holds that humankind is confronted with a self-contradictory experience of death that is rooted deep within the psyche. While the unconscious is convinced of its own immortality, it also finds one of its motive forces, paradoxically, to be the pursuit of death. The coexistence of these two incompatible elements within the unconscious provides an inherent contradiction in human existence. Although a person will struggle to resolve the conflict within, the embracing of one motive force inevitably causes its primal opposite to reassert itself. The human psyche, Borkenau proposes, is caught in a never-ending debate that is a basic element in shaping the course of human history. Furthermore, he argues, the conflicting attitudes toward death unconsciously experienced by the individual are also at work within the culture, so that ultimately there emerge periods when the culture can be characterized as death-denying rather than death-defying.[39]

The attraction of national or social movements, such as communism or fascism, wrapped about as they are with semidivine attributes of absolute value and the promise of a

---

[37] Franz Borkenau, "Concept of Death," *Twentieth Century* 157 (1955): 326.

[38] Borkenau, "Concept of Death," 314–15.

[39] Borkenau, "Concept of Death," 315.

temporal eternity, invite an individual to avoid extinction by an act of self-abandonment. This, Borkenau observes, is also the invitation extended to us by traditional Christian theology. The difference lies in the fact that death-denying cultures seek a form of immortality in this world, in contrast to death-defiant Christianity, which promises everlasting life in the next.[40]

A shift in the popular attitude toward death from one orientation to another serves to mark an epoch in historical evolution. In our time, Borkenau believes, we are experiencing just such a shift.

I would agree with Borkenau that attitudes toward death have changed in modern society, as well as with his observations regarding the direction of that change. I question his explanation for these changes, grounded as it is in the canons of psychoanalytic theory, for which logic and evidence are sorely lacking. I would contend instead that the reversal noted in our collective responses to death is the result of shifts and historical changes within society itself rather than a consequence of unconscious urges or intra-psychic paradoxes that Borkenau—cum Freud—believes bedevil humankind. Rather, technological inventions, scientific discoveries, demographic changes, and other social and cultural factors have served to break the earlier structures and patterns of social life and brought us to our present condition.

---

[40] Borkenau, "Concept of Death," 324.

Chapter 9:
Myth, Mind, and Morality

When we remember we are all mad, the mysteries of life disappear and life stands explained.

–Mark Twain, Notebook, 1898

The human brain, awake or asleep, is a myth maker. In the production of its autonomous mentations, as well as its infinite capacity for fantasy, it weaves—caterpillar-like—a cocoon of mythical beliefs and ideas by which we live and die. Myths provide meaning and purpose in life at the same time that they serve to explain the past even as they portend the future. Myths are neither ancient nor modern—they simply are, integral to our very nature. Contrary to the strongly held conceit that we are rational beings, *Homo sapiens* (wise men), I contend that we should instead acknowledge the ephemeral and chimerical world of myth and accept the designation *Homo mythicus* as a more appropriate definition of our human legacy.

The English social psychologist Roger Needham would concur. He would add to the discussion, however, such primary factors as the polarities that differentiate light from dark, male from female, right from wrong, and right from left—the binary distinctions that are basic to the way the human brain organizes the social world.[1]

Needham argues that there is an important but unexamined connection between public myths and personal dreams that needs to be considered. While Freud explained the dream simply as a product of the mind emanating from a dreamer's id,[2] Needham emphasizes what Freud summarily dismissed. He maintains that the psychic operations found in the dream, such as metamorphoses, levitation, flying, magical powers, illogicalities, and in general all manner of experiences and physical states that are contrary to normal expectations and defy the constraining conditions of reality, can also be recognized in the arena of public myths and social institutions.[3]

Needham observes that the characteristic features of certain public or collective myths—for example, the worldwide belief in witchcraft (or the game of chess)—contain many of the aforementioned mentations. That is, the witch or warlock can metamorphose, fly, transpose herself or himself, cast spells, or cause illness or other manner of harm. Importantly, Needham's observations are consistent with the research on dreaming that has been conducted in the sleep laboratories of neuroscientists.[4]

Neuroscientists have shown that the autonomous waking brain does not necessarily always function rationally but rather moves in and out of a rational state, an observation supported by the investigations of Le Bon and LeShan, as noted earlier, as well as the research on brainwashing conducted by Lifton. The consensus of these several researchers, coming as they do from

---

[1] Rodney Needham, *Primordial Characters* (Charlottesville: University Press of Virginia, 1978), 34.

[2] Freud's term for unconscious wishes and desires.

[3] Needham, *Primordial Characters*, 64.

[4] J. Allan Hobson, *Dreaming: An Introduction to the Science of Sleep* (Oxford: Oxford University Press, 2002).

different disciplines, serves to support the finding that not only can the brain experience an alteration in its cognitive functioning in the dream state, but that an individual's critical faculties can also be compromised in the waking state.

Our willingness to embrace the illogical or the irrational is not only fostered by the mental products of the autonomous, self-actuating brain; it is also reinforced by the human propensity to organize into hierarchical groups and submit to charismatic leadership. Our critical faculties, as has been shown, are susceptible to the natural pressure of the group even as they can be made vulnerable to artificially induced, mind-altering techniques, as Lifton has demonstrated.

These sociological and psychological factors play only a part in the overall culture complex that sustains the belief in immortality. Central to the core of the complex is the Judeo-Christian creation myth that offers the explanation as to why human beings exist and why they die. The paradigm incorporates the cardinal idea from classical Greek philosophy: the concept of a divinely endowed soul that seeks to return to its cosmic creator.

But this belief does not come without a price. Anti-Semitism finds its roots in the Christian belief that Christ is divine and that He has promised his followers that they will, indeed, achieve such a reunion. The historic challenge of Judaism to both of these fundamental Christian beliefs serves as an underlining *cause célèbre* and helps to account for the ancient quarrel between these two religious communities.

Accompanying the idea of the immortal soul, moreover, is the time-honored but misogynous belief that women's souls are of a lesser nature than those of men. The subordinate role that women have historically been obliged to play in Western society (see chapter 3) derives in large part from this egregious canard.

On the other hand, the concept of the soul is a critical idea in Western thought; it is the wellspring of our belief in human equality and the principle of justice—that we are all equal before God.

I would suggest that we may be compelled to invoke what J. Robert Oppenheimer, the physicist, calls the principle of complementarity: that there are some truths that contradict other truths, and one must accept both sets of truths as valid.[5]

In this world in which we find ourselves, we are confronted with a seemingly irresolvable paradox. What is asked of us as individuals as well as members of a modern, secular community is to protect the sanctity of human life and other myth-inspired ideas by supporting, rationally, certain aspects of our mythic legacy that cannot, in and of themselves, be evidentially demonstrated. As the late historian Tony Judt observed, "A well-organized society is one in which we know the truth about ourselves, collectively, not one in which we tell pleasant lies about ourselves."[6]

In response to a growing concern regarding the power of mythic thinking that threatens to lead us today to ever more cataclysmic conflicts and/or ultimately societal suicide, the American psychologist Lawrence LeShan proposes that we make a checklist of specific changes in the way we collectively think and communicate. Such a checklist, he believes, could alert us to the fact that we're either in a state of rational or mythic thought. He suggests that such an evaluation would serve not only to inform us as to how we are thinking about any impending conflict, and whether our mental state is

---

[5] Martin Gardner, ed., *Great Essays in Science* (Amherst, NY: Prometheus Books, 1984), 197.

[6] William Grimes, "Tony Judt, Chronicler of History, Is Dead at 62," *New York Times*, August 8, 2010.

cognitive/rational or mythic/emotional, but it could also help to restrain impetuosity on the one hand or promote action on the other. In the case of the threat of war, for instance, LeShan's proposed checklist includes such questions as: Are we devaluing the potential enemy? Are we dismissing the reasons for the differences between us? Are contrary ideas viewed as disloyal? Is accepted wisdom beyond questioning? Are traditional moral standards being abandoned? Do we judge ourselves differently from the enemy? Are our goals shifting from seeking a solution to promoting a glorious cause?

LeShan suggests that such a checklist might be distributed with some effect if it were publicized under the heading "The Surgeon General has determined that mythical thinking at this time is hazardous to your health and may cause radiation burns and the death of your children."[7]

I would propose a similar checklist be constructed with respect to other important social issues that both confront and confound American society. Such a checklist could assist in mitigating the acrimonious debate over abortion (or stem cell research) that presently embroils the country. The issue of abortion hinges on the mythic belief in the reality of a soul and the related belief that semen is its materialized vehicle. Given such a view, the intentional termination of a fetus is thus viewed as homicide while the denial of procreation by acts of homosexuality, masturbation, or bestiality is seen as sterile lust. Because the soul is denied its rightful existence on the one hand, and the divine gift of life is denigrated on the other, it is believed that God's will is subverted even as He is blasphemed.

What if the soul does not exist, or if it exists, is not contained in semen but rather makes its earthly appearance at the moment of birth by what the Greeks called the pneuma, or the breath of

---

[7] LeShan, *The Psychology of War*, 116.

life? If this idea were embraced, the risk of a moral crime would be avoided while the principle of the sanctity of the soul would be sustained. We now know through scientific research that a woman contributes 50 percent of the genetic inheritance of her child, contrary to what Aristotle taught, and that there is no vessel connecting the brain and the urethra that conveys the soul through semen—the life fluid—as once believed. Moreover, the existence of a soul has never been scientifically demonstrated and continues to be but another unsubstantiated albeit powerful belief among a spectrum of imaginings that make up our mythic legacy. An effort to evaluate the extent, strength, and contemporary acceptance of the belief in the soul could make a significant contribution to the clarification of an issue that continues to haunt the conscience of American society.

Something further needs to be said about the abortion issue, as it goes to the heart of the Judeo-Christian paradigm. Within this worldview, human history is seen as an expression of a divine purpose. Human beings do not make history, nor are they responsible for generating unique events. Rather, such occurrences are viewed as the intentionality of a transcendental being. Earthly events are simply the mechanism by which divine purposes are realized.

The theory of natural law presumes that there is order in the universe and that it is the moral obligation of humans to act in accordance with that order. In his book *Philosophy in the Mass Age,* the Canadian philosopher George Grant asserts that natural law "is the most influential theory of morality in the history of the human race" and is immanent in such civilizations as Greece, Rome, India, and China.[8] It was dominant in Western

---

[8] George Grant, *Philosophy in the Mass Age* (Toronto, ON: University of Toronto Press, 1995), 26.

societies until the last two hundred years, when it was seriously challenged by both the concept of human progress and the Cartesian revolution in science. Importantly, the theory of natural law continues to remain the keystone of the Roman Catholic Church.[9]

The doctrine of natural law contends that the universe is a harmonious system—a cosmos—not chaos. It is held together by reason, the same reason that we presume we share with God, that allows for the conceit of designating ourselves *Homo sapiens*. It is an order in which all things have their place: plants, animals, human beings, angels, and ultimately, the creator of all things—God—who is reason, harmony, and order personified. The universe is thus believed to be a great chain of being, moved by extraterrestrial law, and ruled by the divine mind.[10]

The nature of anything, Grant explains, "is that which it is when it realizes its immanent meaning, that is, when it takes its proper place in the whole."[11]

This ancient view of the universe must be understood if we are to comprehend the moral principles that are derived from it. The belief in moral law, Grant argues, depends ultimately on how we understand the movement of the stars. He contends that if we deny that their motion is the result of a first cause or the mind of God, we can eventually deny that there is any reason or law governing human life, and thus any basis for human morality. Basically, the doctrine of natural law rests on the assumption that metaphysical knowledge can be acquired and that true judgments can be made about the order of the universe, causality, and God. To assert, however, that there is a final cause to the motion of the planets is not to say that this is a

---

9 Grant, *Philosophy in the Mass Age*, 26.
10 Grant, *Philosophy in the Mass Age*, 28.
11 Grant, *Philosophy in the Mass Age*, 28.

scientific or rational explanation of the phenomenon; rather, Grant insists, it is only by affirming that there is metaphysical knowledge that we can speak of natural law, thereby allowing us to deduce the principles of right action in human affairs.[12]

In ancient and preliterate societies, all-important activities such as farming, fishing, hunting, and art, as well as the act of human copulation, were made holy by sacerdotal invocation. Human action was believed to have meaning insofar as it represented a divine act, one that was incumbent upon us to repeat endlessly.[13]

While human acts were accepted as imitations of the original, they were nevertheless possessed of the sacred and thus acquired a religious significance. The belief is immanent in Christian liturgy, in which Christ's birth, passion, and resurrection are observed annually, while His sacrifice is reenacted daily in the Catholic Mass. In the observance of this divine act, endlessly repeated, the meaninglessness of existence is overcome, and the transcendent vision of life ever after affirmed.

Human justice in ancient societies mirrored this transcendental model, while the law upon which it was based was presumed to preexist written law. Human laws, therefore, incorporated the doctrine of natural law and ultimately became the basis of our legal and moral codes. What is right conforms to natural law; what is wrong does not.

The doctrine of natural law makes certain assumptions about the nature of human nature and how one should conduct one's life. It assumes that human nature is ultimately the same everywhere and that to be human is to possess a rational soul, for that is what distinguishes humans from animals in the

---

[12] Grant, *Philosophy in the Mass Age*, 31.
[13] Grant, *Philosophy in the Mass Age*, 17.

hierarchy of the great chain of being. As a consequence, we have the intelligence to make choices and to determine for ourselves what is good and proper. Importantly, the discovery of proper ends must be made through reflection and education.[14] Wisdom, the condition that humans can reach through reason, is the true purpose of education, for it is through rational thought that we come to know what purposes in human life are worthy. To live according to the precepts of natural law is to realize the supreme good for humankind. In doing so, we are brought to our highest potential through union with divine reason.[15]

Natural law operates in the personal moral decisions of life, as well as in the laws of the state. A case in point, previously discussed, is the continuing issue of abortion. While many people view abortion as a private decision and a personal act that should be available whenever one chooses, supporters of natural law view abortion as morally wrong, since they contend that it is not within the dominion of another person to extinguish what is believed to be a human life. In this view, the sanctity of life is the law of nature, and as Grant observes, it is a law that we did not make nor one that we can alter without contravening God's will.[16] Moral conduct, rationally understood, is not a matter of convenience; rather it is incumbent upon us to actualize the eternal law in our own lives.

For many, such a worldview is no longer acceptable. It is considered both wrong-headed and alien to humankind's higher aspirations. The idea that we gain our human identity through repetition of, or participation in, a divine reality is unsupportable. As Grant observes, modern-day, secularly minded individuals insist in taking their fate into their own

---

[14] Grant, *Philosophy in the Mass Age*, 29.
[15] Grant, *Philosophy in the Mass Age*, 30.
[16] Grant, *Philosophy in the Mass Age*, 31.

hands and are determined to make the world as they want it. As he states, "We and not God are the creators of history. Unique and irreversible events must be shaped by creative acts of human will."[17]

The nineteenth-century English reformer Jeremy Bentham also argued for this point of view. He scorned the idea of divine law because it placed both the law and events outside of human control. For Bentham, the only law is that created by humans, and it is only through their conscious acts that the world is shaped and goals realized.[18]

But the proponents of natural law challenge this argument by insisting that the right way to live can only be deduced from the unchanging law that is both the reason and will of God. Moral relativity, they contend, is the path along which can be found the belief that there are lives "not worth living" culminating, as the world has witnessed, in the bottomless horror that was Auschwitz. They contend that the supreme good is for humankind to live according to nature where we are brought to our highest possibility through the union of human reason with divine reason. As the English jurist Blackstone observed, "This law of nature being co-eval with mankind and dictated by God, Himself, is of course superior in obligation to any other. It is binding over the whole globe in all countries at all times. No human laws are of any validity if contrary to this and such of them as are valid derive their force and all their authority, mediately or immediately, from this original."[19]

Simply put, positive laws are the laws that men enact, but they are only legitimate to the extent that they are consistent with the laws of God. The idea of a fair trial, for instance, is

---

[17] Grant, *Philosophy in the Mass Age*, 37.

[18] Grant, *Philosophy in the Mass Age*, 47.

[19] Grant, *Philosophy in the Mass Age*, 30.

integral to a just system of law, as is the belief that all persons have certain rights that cannot be denied them or taken away at the caprice of others, whether they be a dictatorial government or a democracy.

Being mythmakers, however, does not mean that we have to be mischief makers or that all myths necessarily lead us down the road to mindlessness or madness. Charity (chapter 6) is a most worthwhile and beneficial activity, based as it is on the belief of a loving God and His commandment, "Love thy neighbor as thyself." Moreover, it is not a practice that we should readily abandon, given its proven usefulness and its promulgation of the altruistic ideal. Those who would subvert the act of charity and exploit it for their own private benefit threaten to undermine an important social cohesive.

Reason, however, much as it is ignored in the world, is still our most powerful defense against greed and other human follies. While I believe we will never divest ourselves of our own nature, we can, through reason, curb or control our misanthropic impulses and those myth-based beliefs that have shown to be divisive, debilitating, or deadly. Charity is not such a belief. To the contrary, it is both a personal and community-sustaining activity that deserves our most ardent support despite its mythic origins. LeShan's proposal, therefore, for a checklist concerning our mental state as we address the different social issues that continually challenge us has the potential of mitigating or correcting harmful behavior.

The American public, for example, recently expressed its revulsion for the racist remarks made by the popular radio and television personality Don Imus. He was subsequently censored and ultimately dismissed from his show. Importantly, a national debate ensued that had the beneficial effect of significantly raising the public's consciousness with respect to the harm that words can inflict. Just as the country was able to diffuse much of Imus' demeaning and injurious comments, so, too, must we be prepared to challenge the errant speech or behavior of those who would do similar harm.

We have witnessed in the past few years two presidents of the United States who have described other nations as "evil"— the very kind of demonizing speech found in Imus's remarks and of which LeShan cautions us. Such pejorative expressions do nothing to advance racial understanding or the political goals or the moral aspirations of a country. To the contrary, such words serve merely to distance one people from another and invite further misunderstanding and conflict.

The most far-reaching example of the mythic tradition is the Christian belief in immortality. On the one hand, it is ultimately reassuring: not only does it promise the individual that he or she will not die, but it also offers assurance that family members and friends will be reunited forever in the afterlife. But on the other hand, the threat of eternal punishment—of spiritual separation from God—hangs like the sword of Damocles over the head of every guiltless child.

It is true that over time it has been shown that objective, evidential knowledge has and will compel change in both what we think and do, whether the change is necessarily welcomed or not. Medical science was compelled to abandon the theories of Hippocrates and Galen regarding systemic illness and the humors that dominated the thinking of the Western medical world for more than two millennia, as a result of Pasteur's experimentally based germ theory of disease. In like manner, it should be remembered that reason has triumphed over myth in different areas of life. We no longer burn heretics at the stake, nor hang witches, nor, since the passage of the Eighth Amendment to the Constitution, do we permit "cruel and unusual punishment," despite recent events to the contrary.

On the other hand, it must be recognized that the belief in immortality represents a tradition of thought that is both prior to, and separate from, the conscious psychological and sociological experiences of an eschatological nature that have been reported over the centuries. The belief that there is ultimately no death—that in some way, somewhere, human existence continues—originates primarily as a result of the innate way the autonomous brain functions and that is reaffirmed anew in the idiosyncratic dreams of each succeeding generation.

Whatever the ultimate truth may be with respect to the genesis of the belief in immortality, it is important to recognize that humankind has denied the finality of death well before the historical appearance of Moses, Buddha, Jesus, or Muhammad, and the other avatars who have contributed to the mythic beliefs and spiritual foundations of the world. What this implies, of course, is that no matter what the nature or extent of the decline of our religious legacy might be, or the role that reason may ultimately come to play in human affairs, the belief in immortality—the belief in the endlessness of self—will persist.

Index

Acknowledgments

When I began my sociological research into the multiple effects that death presents both society and the individual in the 1950s, little did I realize that a half century later I would be examining its antonym—immortality. In 1958, I published an article (with William Faunce) entitled "The Sociology of Death: A Neglected Area of Research." In connection with that project, we read Sigmund Freud's classic paper "Mourning and Melancholia," in which he advocated that grieving survivors should work through their loss by detaching themselves emotionally from the deceased. Over time, I came to realize just how difficult and perhaps impossible Freud's proposal was, given the general expression of the belief in an afterlife and the reported experiences of communicating with the dead through dreams and other social and psychic avenues. Over the years, I was to learn that continued contact with the dead is not necessarily an unwelcome event; indeed, it is often reported to be a comforting experience while the hope of reuniting with the deceased is a warmly anticipated and much welcomed prospect. This book represents the culmination of my professional involvement in this intriguing issue.

I would like to acknowledge the support of my colleagues for their careful perusal of earlier drafts of the book. Thanks are due to Ira Reiss, Joel Nelson, and David Kopf of the University of Minnesota. Ira Reiss, in particular, needs to be recognized for his friendship and astute counsel over the intervening years. Inge Corless, of the Massachusetts General Hospital Institute, also lent her professional expertise in reviewing the book as well as her support as a longtime friend.

The members of the Lake Owen Book Club read and discussed an early version of the book. Their comments and observations were extremely helpful. Sincere thanks are due to Patrick Clyne, Bruce Hendry, Erwin Kelen, Ross Kimmerle, Byron Olsen, John Rollwagen, John Soucheray, and Tom Warth.

This book is also the product of numerous discussions and professional exchanges that I have had over five decades with colleagues who have shared my interest in the issues of death and immortality. Their knowledge and insights are reflected in many of the pages of this book. I owe a debt of gratitude, in particular, to William Lamers Jr., Herman Feifel, Cicely Saunders, Inge Corless, Edgar Jackson, Earl Grollman, William Faunce, Hannelore Wass, Leif Wahlstrom, Marie Louise Wahlstrom, Tom Stewart, Roger Rudolph, Gendron Jensen, Greg Owen, and Eric Markusen.

My secretarial staff—Mary Drew, Samantha Kennedy, Susan Dunn, and Valerie Graser—need to be acknowledged for their efforts and diligence throughout the long winter-like struggle to bring the manuscript to press. Mary Drew, I must say, has not only been a friend and assistant for over twenty years, but her significant contributions to the text and her editorial skills added appreciably to the content of the book as well as to its exposition.

I would like to express my sincere thanks to my editor, Ann Staton of American Book Publishing. Her enthusiastic endorsement of the book and her unstinting efforts to bring it to fruition are deeply appreciated. My appreciation is also extended to Jana Rade, Director of Design, for her stunning cover design.

I want to acknowledge the loving support that Meryl Baker extended to me over the past few years. Her forbearance through the many readings of the manuscript would serve as an example for any aspiring martyr.

Finally, I would like to thank the Baywood Publishing Company Inc. for permission to quote from my articles, "When Death Took a Holiday," in *Illness, Crisis and Loss* 11, no. 1 (2003): 47–64, and "Death and Society in Twentieth Century America" from *OMEGA—Journal of Death and Dying* 8, no. 4 (1987–88): 379–95; Springer Publishing Company, , for "Society and the Imperative of Death," in *Dying, Death and Bereavement,* edited by I. B. Corless, B. Germino, and M. Pittman, 1993, pp. 61–79; Jason Aronson, Inc., for "Death, Society, and the Quest for Immortality," in *Death and the Quest for Meaning,* edited by Stephen Strack, 1997, pp. 329–44.

About the Author

Robert Fulton is professor of sociology (emeritus) at the University of Minnesota. He is the founder and director (emeritus) of the Center for Death Education and Research. He taught the first college course on the subject of death in the United States at the university in 1963. In 1965 he edited the book *Death and Identity*, and in 1970 was the co-founder and first associate editor of *Omega—Journal of Death and Dying*. In 1978, he edited the book *Death and Dying: Challenge and Change*, in conjunction with the Course by Newspaper Project, which he coordinated under the auspices of the National Endowment for the Humanities. In 1985, Dr. Fulton was the recipient of the Outstanding Achievement Award presented by the National Forum for Death Education and Counseling; in 1990 the Sociological Practice Association honored him with their Distinguished Career Award; in 2008 he received the Herman Fiefel Award from the International Work Group on Death, Grief, and Bereavement. He has been a visiting professor at Osmania University, Hyderabad, India; University of Cape Town, Cape Town, South Africa; St. Luke's College, Tokyo, Japan; and Nankai University, Tianjin, China. He also served as a visiting research professor at Rode Kors Sykehjem, Bergen,

.1umhemmet, Karolinska Institute, Stockholm,
.d St. Christopher's Hospice, London, England.

.olications

Death and Identity, (ed.), (New York: John Wiley and Sons, 1965).

Death and Identity, (ed.), revised edition (Bowie, Maryland: Robert J. Brady Co., 1976).

Death and Identity, with Robert Bendiksen (eds.), 3rd Edition, (Philadelphia, PA: The Charles Press, 1994).

Death, Grief and Bereavement: Bibliography II, 1975-1980, with Margaret Reed (ed.), (New York: Arno Press, 1981).

Death and Dying: Challenge and Change, with Jane Scheiber, Greg Owen and Eric Markusen (eds.), (New York: Addison-Wesley, 1978).

Death, Grief and Bereavement: A Bibliography, 1845-1975, (ed.), (New York: Arno Press, 1976).

Education and Social Crisis: Perspectives on Teaching Disadvantaged Youth, with Everett Keach and William Gardner (eds.), (New York: John Wiley and Sons, 1967).